"Amy, you are truly special in every way. I admire your intelligence and your strength. You have a kindness deep within your soul that can't be explained but it radiates through your words. Thank you for sharing them with us."

—Carolyn Baldwin

"You have made me realize through your writing how much of my life I still haven't lived. I haven't experienced anything… Why do I just simply live life and not become a part of it? Thank you for sharing that with me."

—Mark Iannuzzo

"I want to thank you for the beautiful vignettes you have been sharing from your life in Italy. When I am reading your letters I feel completely transported to Italy, to your world there. I find your writing to be very soothing, inspiring, descriptive… like a mini vacation."

—Julie "CJ" Johnson

"The particular story and the details of "scoping" literally, and I do mean literally, almost made me pee my pants laughing to myself. You are a great story teller."

—Monica Tijerias

The Sights, Sounds, and Silences of Italy

The Sights, Sounds, and Silences of Italy

◆

Reflections and Observations from My Time Abroad

Amy Szarkowski

iUniverse, Inc.

New York Lincoln Shanghai

The Sights, Sounds, and Silences of Italy
Reflections and Observations from My Time Abroad

iUniverse, Inc.

For information address:
iUniverse, Inc.
2021 Pine Lake Road, Suite 100
Lincoln, NE 68512
www.iuniverse.com

ISBN: 0-595-29665-3

Printed in the United States of America

Contents

Introduction

This book began as a collection of "letters to home" in the form of email messages to friends keeping them updating them about my travels and adventures in Italy. It changed over the course of my time abroad, and became more of a memoir, a place for me to share the things I saw and the ways in which those things changed me. Somewhere along the way, I received feedback from several people, saying, "You know, you should publish your letters. They are really good." I have decided to take a chance that they might be right.

My experiences in Italy resulted from my opportunity to live and work as a Fulbright student in Rome for the spring of 2003. At the time of this writing, I was a doctoral student in clinical psychology at Gallaudet University, focusing my studies on working with families with deaf children. I had completed my coursework and defended my dissertation, and I was off to do a Fulbright exchange before returning to the States for my last year of training and thus the completion of my Ph.D. This book is about what happened "in between."

With Thanks

These experiences would not have been possible without the opportunity afforded by the Italian Fulbright Commission, the United States Fulbright Commission, the Italian National Research Council (CNR) which sponsored my work, and more specifically to Cristina Caselli and Virginia Volterra, who agreed to host me and provided me with guidance in my work. Thanks also to Elena Raduzky, who served as my advisor in Rome and truly made this opportunity possible for me. A huge thanks to Cristina from Brazil, my confidant and friend who shared the living abroad experience with me, and taught me much about resiliency and life. Paolo, I am filled with gratitude for showing me the Italian Deaf Culture and for being so kind. To Marianna, my true Italian friend who shared her life, her family, and her insights with me in order that I might fully experience "la bella vita." She made the phrase "When in Rome, do as the Romans do" a reality for me. I am deeply and forever indebted to these individuals for granting me the chance of a lifetime.

I would not have been able to have these experiences were it not for the individuals that guided me along the way. To my teachers—thank you for encouraging me and making learning so much a part of my life. To my friends—thank you for sharing with me the good, the bad, the exciting, the scary, and everything in-between. To everyone in my family, especially "The Ma" and "Daddy-O"—thank you for loving me unconditionally, for putting up with my "permanent student status," and for teaching me that I could do what I wanted with my life. Your belief in me was sometimes stronger than my belief in myself. You let me know that whatever it was, I could do it. Thank you for that gift.

1

The Opportunity of a Lifetime

The call came at 5 a.m. on a morning I wasn't expecting it. It was the Italian representative for the Italian Fulbright Commission. She wanted to talk to me about my application and ask me "further questions." She also wanted to judge my commitment to learning a language, and at one point suggested we continue this additional interview in Italian. I reminded her that I had only had one Italian class (in fact I had just begun it at the time of the call), but promised that my language skills would improve and that I would be able to do the project I proposed, should they choose to give me a Fulbright to live in Italy. I could learn a language. I would learn a language, if it meant going to Italy...

The email arrived a few days later. I was going to Italy! Although I am a grown person, and typically would call myself "mature," I was jumping up and down, yelling to roommate to "come and look at this" on my computer screen and hugging her until she did not know what to do. I asked her to pinch me. She did. I didn't feel it. But she assured me that it wasn't a dream.

I had gambled a lot on the possibility that I might be "one of the chosen ones." In my Ph.D. program at Gallaudet University in Washington, D.C., I had completed my coursework and was in a position to apply for an internship position, which would have allowed me to graduate one year earlier. With the timing of things, I could not apply for both the Fulbright and an internship position and see what happened. I needed to determine what I really wanted to do and go for it. The decision was made easier by telling myself, "I need a break from school anyway. Even if I don't get this, I will still have a good year," but telling myself and believing it where two different things. I decided that I wanted to go overseas, that I needed an experience of living in another country, and that I believed I was "qualified"—the latter only after talking to several people and being convinced that I had a shot. I had put myself out there, given it a try, and it felt at that moment as if my dreams were coming true.

The months that followed the phone conversation and the email were strange to say the least. In two months time, I completed my dissertation and defended it. I moved all of my belongings into a 5x7 crate, and sold everything that wouldn't fit. I quit the job I had only had for a short time, breaking a commitment, though they considered Rome "a good excuse." I said good-bye to loved ones, friends, and everything that I knew in the place that I had called home. The Fulbright was not to begin until January, but in keeping with my promise to learn the language (the one course I had been taking didn't quite do it for me), I went to Italy on my own to study Italian and learn about the culture. I spent an amazing couple of months, first in Sienna, and then in Florence, learning everything about Italy and Italian that I could soak in as I went along. I left D.C. not knowing when I would come back. Since I had postponed my internship, I would need to fly back to the U.S. to interview for positions in December, and then head to Rome to officially begin this adventure. I wouldn't know until March where I would be placed. In leaving Washington, I left what had been my home, knowing that I wouldn't return, but not knowing what that would mean for me at the time, and not knowing where I might return. I was off to live in a foreign country and work in a language I barely knew. My feelings ranged from excited to scared, to amazed, to overwhelmed, to thrilled and giddy and lonely and sad. To say that this was a big change would be an understatement. To say it was the opportunity of a lifetime would be just about right.

In order to help you understand how I perceived my experience in Italy, I think you need to know a thing or two about me. Many of my qualities, I guess you could call them quirks, if you wanted to, influenced how I interpreted the things that happened to me overseas. Humor me and let me tell you how I see myself. Those who know me might disagree, but you would have to ask them personally.

I am a people person. I enjoy meeting new people, and interacting with people who are not like me, as I assume they usually have something to teach me, if I allow them to do so. People fascinate me and I strive to make important connections. I am also extremely solitary in some of my endeavors. I enjoy my alone time and I need time to myself to relax and to rejuvenate. It is when I am alone that I feel most spiritual, when in the company of others that I feel most appreciative of the life I have had an opportunity to lead.

My decisions tend to be based on thought, analyses, and pro-con lists, and I follow that up with mostly listening to my intuition. I believe that when I do that, I don't go wrong. The analytical part of me enjoys the intellectual challenge of figuring things out and that makes me observant. The emotional part of me wants to connect with others and to make a difference in people's lives, which allows me to be a participant. I like to think that the combination of these things make me good at what I do—therapeutic work with children and families, Deaf children in particular.

I am fascinated with Sign Language, with the beauty of conveying thoughts through space using one's body. I enjoy the interplay involved in working with people who have different experiences than I. Those who cannot hear find so many others ways to enjoy their world is interesting to me. It is beautiful. I am passionate.

I have been told that I am driven. I prefer to call it "goal-oriented." Call it what you will, I do tend to set goals and to go after them. I don't always achieve, but I also don't have regrets for lack of trying. Related to this is my independence. That is an interesting adjective when describing women in today's world, I believe. The same word can be pronounced with pride or envy or pity or misunderstanding. Why would you want to be independent? For me, it has something to do with freedom. That doesn't mean lack of relationships, rather, it means fully being who I am and doing what I need and want to do so that I can be truly myself in relationships. I see it as a positive thing, but I do know that it requires patience on the part of the people in my life.

My moral code guides my actions. It is sometimes difficult to articulate what it is and from where that code is derived. It has many roots. My way of living isn't the "right way," but I do believe that it is right for me. And being the analytical person that I am, I have given that some thought. I have voiced my opinions throughout this text. I know that not everyone will agree with everything that I have said. I don't expect them to, nor would I want that. The world and its citizens are diverse. That keeps it interesting. Please know that my stance in these pages reflects where I was at that moment. Since I believe in continuing growth and reflection, I reserve the right to change my mind.

The final aspect of my character that I will share with you is my desire to live in the moment. In my daily experience of life on this planet, I strive to cherish the small stuff, the "what is happening right now" in front of me. Writing about my experiences in Rome helped me to do that. Sending letters to friends and keeping my journal were ways for me to cherish the moments and reflect on the nuances of life in a foreign country. By reading this, you are helping me to share that.

The entries in this text are made up of my thoughts along the way. They were taken from my laptop journal, and my emails to friends back in the States. This writing represents my reactions to things as they happened, at this special time in my life while I was living in Rome. Please join me as I relive this journey through time and space and Italy.

What should this writing be?

I have been struggling recently with what I want this writing to be. I am not exactly sure. At first, I thought I would simply send out some highlights of my trip to Italy, but the more I write, the more I want to also create a balanced picture. Initially, I thought this "journaling" would be of benefit for you, my friends, to get to see some of the experiences that I am having that my pictures just won't be able to capture. However, as of late, I am learning that this writing is more for me. It is nice to have a small audience of interested friends and family, but this has become a vehicle for making sense of my experiences here. I have kept various journals over the years, mostly in times of need or sadness. Those journals contain poems and quotes and many emotions. I still have, in the nightstand next to my bed, a journal that I write in occasionally at night before going to bed and frequently take with me on hiking trips, when I am inspired by nature and beauty. But lately, I feel the need to type—to write my thoughts at a pace much closer to that of my thinking than my handwriting will allow. I need to express what I am feeling, to allow myself to put into words the emotions to which I have been stirred because of the experiences I have had. This is becoming less of a beautiful memoir of Italy, and more of a story of my life in a new place. It is now more about me and less about you. For anyone not interested in that aspect, feel free to stop here. If you are willing to follow me on this journey to where ever it is that it takes me, please read on.

2

Initial Impression/Rome at First Glance

I landed in Rome on Sunday evening, and began my work the next day. My roommate, whom I did not know, though I had met once, met me at the airport to assist me in finding my new home. She had, luckily, done the legwork, and got us an apartment in the center of Rome. I was taken with Rome immediately. It did not feel like home, but it was a place that could be home to me someday.

My first week

As I write this, it is Sunday morning, and I am sitting at the window in my apartment, overlooking the old tower in the center of the piazza on which I now live. I have been in Rome one week as of today. Wow—what a week it has been. I arrived in the afternoon last Sunday and found my way to my new residence. I like it! The apartment has two bedrooms and two bathrooms, as well as a big open room that is the kitchen, living space and dining room. It has two daybeds that serve as couches and are actually comfortable. We have a washing machine right in the kitchen area, which makes me happy, as not many apartments in Rome have them. My roommate, Linda, had been here for a week before I got here, so I had the benefit of having some necessities already stocked, like toilet paper and dish soap. We had dinner at the pizzeria on the corner—a great mushroom pizza. It is hard to describe how nice it was to unpack. I have been living out of suitcases since the end of October, three months with just my two bags. I didn't mind it—I traveled all over and had a chance to visit family, it was great. However, it was nice to put my things in their place and make it my own. My bedroom window faces an old tower, dedicated to Saint Martin of the Mountains. I am not sure of his story yet, but I intend to find out more.

My first full day was Fulbright orientation—8 hours of it, which was a bit tough with my jetlag. It was interesting and informational, and a nice start to living here. I learned a lot of the basics of Roman life, as well as the organization of the Fulbright commission and the Mason Perkins Deafness Fund, which is sponsoring me here. I also got to meet the whole group of people that I will be working with, and my first impression was that they were nice and welcoming. I decided that it was going to be GREAT working there! I came home and went directly to bed—and slept for 10 hours.

On Tuesday, I met the psychologists that I will be working with in the morning and went with them to a large meeting. They work for the CNR (Cosiglieare Nazionale di Richerce)—the National Research Council—in the Division of Neuropsychology and Linguistics. I met leading researchers from all over Italy at this meeting and attended several sessions. In the morning, I was concentrating hard and reading the slide presentations they had. I was able to follow pretty well—even though they all seem to speak so fast! Admittedly, it helped that I was familiar with the topics that they covered. My research group discussed their recent findings with deaf children, and I had previously read their work. By the afternoon, though, I realized just how much effort I was exerting into understanding the language. I blanked out; I couldn't even remember what those last two sessions were about. That evening, I walked around my neighborhood and explored a bit. I live very near the Chiesa di Maria Maggiore—which is one of four basilicas in Rome. Not that there aren't many other Catholic churches...

My first real day of working was interesting. We had a staff meeting and I got to meet other people that work at the CNR. My office mate, Paolo, is a deaf man who communicates using LIS (Italian Sign Language), though he is familiar with ASL (American Sign Language). He has been told to only use LIS with me. I have a very large LIS dictionary at my desk, so I look things up before asking him questions. I think this is a great opportunity, and look forward to learning this language. I have the Italian alphabet down, so even if I don't know a sign, I can spell it to him—provided I know the Italian word for what I want, and how to spell it!

Exploring my new home

I have been going for runs in the mornings and find that is one of my favorite times of the day and one of my favorite things about being in Rome. I love to explore on foot and see where I end up. If you go up one block from my apartment building, you can see the coliseum! It is amazing to me that it is right there!

Even though you can see it, you must first go through this amazing park to get there. In the park there are many orange trees in full bloom. They produce blood oranges—that really look like they have veins running through them. I had previously tried the juice from these, which is red, but I ate my first blood orange this week and really liked it. The park is covered with ancient ruins. It was only after I got through the park and down to the coliseum that I realized that what I had been running on was a park that was built on top of the old cells where the Roman gladiators had trained. Thank goodness I watched PBS in D.C.; I learned a lot about Rome from their weekend specials on travel—so I recognized this place. It gave me a weird feeling, knowing that many gladiators died in those cells.

On Thursday, good news arrived via email. I had submitted a proposal for the European Congress on Deafness and Mental Health, which will take place in Austria in May. They have accepted the proposal to present the findings of the work that I will be doing here in Rome with the families of deaf children. I talked with the Fulbright office, and it seems they are willing to pay my expenses, which would then allow me to go. That is incentive to get my project done on time!! I will be duplicating my dissertation with the Italian population—although the transcribing will probably take much longer.

I spent Friday working in the office, and typing my first memo in Italian. I must say, it took a while. Knowing some vocabulary is one thing, putting it all together with the correct grammar and the appropriate tense is another matter! There is another woman in the CNR who is a "part-timer"—she is from Brazil and her primary language is Portuguese. She has lived in Italy for a time before, but it was many years ago. Her Italian is still far better than mine, but we both know what it is like to be here as a foreigner. I very much enjoy her company at work. She is trying to learn English, so I agreed to help her out in that area.

Along the lines of learning languages—I had my first LIS class on Friday! I had indicated that I wanted to learn and asked if there was someone at the office willing to teach me. They are all more than happy to help me if I have specific questions but are busy with their own work. So—I joined a class that is in progress. The class members were friendly and wanted to learn more about ASL and the Deaf Culture in America. I learned a ton in that one class and now look forward to going twice a week. It is taught in the same building as the CNR and it starts right after I get off work, so it will be easy for me to attend. The teacher is a Deaf Italian who is very good at what she does. Though I am at a disadvantage by not knowing a lot of the vocabulary, I do know many of the classifiers and facial expressions that the class is having difficulty learning. I think we will all be able to help each other. I am excited about that, and about knowing LIS well enough to effectively communicate with Paolo and the other deaf folks that are involved in the research projects that I am working on.

Yesterday was Saturday. I woke up and went out without a plan. I just walked wherever it looked appealing and "discovered" things that I didn't know where there. Although I had been to Rome for 2 days a few years ago and saw some of the "highlights," this was better. I was finding things that I would not have seen if I were looking for something, they would have been bypassed. This is one of my favorite things about traveling solo—I really love to just explore and see where it takes me. Sometimes I see amazing things that I want to share with others, but the experience of going solo and spending as much time, or as little, on certain things has great appeal. I will have to take lots of pictures of these places and share them with the folks back home that way. And now I have ideas of where to take some of the guests who might visit me here in Rome!

It was such a beautiful day yesterday, very chilly and yet sunny. With the exception of one large bus of Japanese tourists, I didn't see any other tourists throughout the day, until I accidentally arrived at the Chiesa di San Pietro (Church of St. Peter—also known as the Vatican). I am sure that being anywhere in Rome during the late spring or summer months would be very different, but I felt like one of the "crowd." I treated myself to lunch at a very quaint place, and had Frutti di Mare (Fruit of the Sea)—which is big crusty bread with seafood on top. It was delicious.

This morning I ran again and found another park near my house, in the other direction. I ran at sunrise, so there were no people out. I like weekends. I like my work here too, don't get me wrong, but there is something very neat about living here and not only visiting here that makes these jaunts more relaxing. I don't feel the need to squeeze it all in. If I see things that are interesting, I can make a mental note of it and plan to return, rather than feeling as if it is "now or never." On the other hand, I know that I will only be living here a short time, so I still want to make the most of all of the time that I have here.

3

Unique Experiences of a Fulbright Student

Being a Fulbright Student

During my first week in Rome, I attended a meeting with all of the other Fulbright students in Italy. I met Americans from all over the U.S. who were also given the opportunity to come to Italy. We met for two days and were "wined and dined" by the Fulbright Commission, as we presented our projects and gave progress reports. What a fascinating group of people! There are several artists (this being Italy, I expected that), who are all doing interesting projects on sculptor, printmaking, and painting in addition to art history, and the study of opera and musicology. I also met a medical student who is narrowing down the search for the reason that Alzheimer's patients have more plague in their brains, a law student who is studying the impact of the establishment of the European Union on American judicial law, a creative writer who is studying Italian literature, a filmmaker who is filming "The history of cappuccino" (a documentary on the "Starbuck-ness" of American culture vs. the small café culture of Italy) and an environmental scientist who is studying how Italy uses gray water in an effort to develop international rules governing how we dispose of water that we have used once before. There was one other psychology student as well, doing a comparative study on the memory of Italians and Americans. This was the first year Italy accepted psychology students, so we were happy to see the each other there. I felt honored, privileged, excited, and motivated by meeting this group.

The Vice-President of Italy

As part of this two-day workshop, we were given a special tour of the Senate Building in Rome. It is not open to the public, and has not traditionally given tours to groups such as ours. I have read some about Italian politics, but since it has 10 parties, it can be quite difficult to remember it all without context. However, being there made a strong impression on me and I found it beautiful. The equivalent of the Vice-President of Italy spoke to us, Professore Marcello Pera, Presidente del Senato della Repubblica Italiana. It was one of those graduation-type speeches…"You are the future…you can change the world…. We are passing on the torch…" He was quite dynamic and interesting, and had agreed to the tour because he himself is a former Fulbright student who went to the U.S. 40 years ago.

The press was there and took many photos. I was front and center for the photo op. with Seniore Pera, with his arm around me. He told me he picked me to be there because of my smile. I smiled for hours after that, whether his statement was true or not. It was an interesting experience; one I don't think I will ever forget.

The U.S Ambassador to Italy

After the amazing tour of the Italian senate, we were treated to a cocktail hour at a famous hotel in Rome. When I got the Fulbright, they said I would be a "U.S. representative." At the time, I didn't realize that I would be asked to actually talk to Italian and American department heads about the U.S.! I was seated at the table of the U.S. Ambassador to Italy and his wife, as well as their out of town guests. The entire evening felt a bit surreal. I am not used to fancy parties, cocktail hours where formal attire is required, and meetings where women wear jewelry that shines in your eyes and nearly blinds you.

My favorite person at this reception was "Babs." She was the friend of the ambassador's wife, and was perhaps the most elegantly (i.e. expensively) dressed woman I have ever seen. Her "hello blue" eyeshadow went up past where her eyebrows should have been, had they not been plucked completely out many years ago. She was an amazing conversationalist. As I watched her do a check-in with each person at the table, she was somehow able to relate each person's work to something in her own life. She remembered every name and every topic area of study of all of the students that she met. Since the ambassador is a political appointee, they were all friends of George W. Close friends. They are rich, close friends from Texas. The men all served in the service together, and the wives all met when they were in their early 20s.

Babs continually told us we were smart, that she admired what we were doing, and that she had never studied hard or even really worked a day in her life. She did this in such a way that she made you feel good, while also making you wonder how in the world other folks in the world can get by without working at all. Babs was interesting and entertaining. She was the depiction of what I never want to become, yet I liked her immensely. Through all the pretentiousness, she was far more real than the other political figures in the room. Babs "accidentally" drank too much, snorted when she laughed, and had food stuck in her teeth when the evening was all over. Back to my theme of "We are all really the same, if we only see past our differences."

I enjoyed myself that evening. After the cocktail hour, I went to a pub with some of my new friends from around Italy and chatted about Italian music; what life is like in Bologna, Venice, and Naples; the happy hour specials; the struggles we have with the language; and the desire all of us have for Thai food. I was once again felt "grounded."

Mr. Fulbright's Big Night

Last night I attended the retirement party for Luigi Filipora. He has been the executive director of the Italian Fulbright Commission for 53 years. I am trying to comprehend 53 years, and cannot even begin to imagine what it would be to work on a project for such a great length of time. Luigi is "Mr. Fulbright"—he exudes niceness and I like him very much. I first met Luigi at the training workshop I attended several weeks ago. He joined all the students on their tour of Tivoli and the waterfalls. He is cute, always smiling, with a great laugh that comes from deep inside and is not adjusted for the sake of whatever situation he might find himself in. Luigi was presented a plague from the U.S. embassy, and several notes were read aloud that had been written by diplomats and various other important people that I did not know (secretary of the U.S. Department of this or that, Italian government officials, etc.). You know what I most enjoyed? It was watching the look on his face when these kind words were said about him. Luigi cried, which of course made many of us in the room cry. To be a part of a project that one believes in, to contribute to the growth and development of something that is very important to you, to look back on the accomplishments of a lifetime—a powerful thing.

I mentioned that members of the Embassy where there—yep, all of them. I also met a 93 year-old woman who sponsors a Fulbright from Italy to the U.S. in fashion. She still walks everyday, works several days a week at her fashion industry, drives her own car, and makes fun of aging men (she figures she has the right, after all, there were no men there older than she). I enjoyed talking with this woman, and admired her grace.

I think I can mingle OK. I am typically a decent conversationalist. I can listen, and since most people in those social situations just really want to be able to talk about themselves, the listening serves me well. Yet, I don't know that this type of gig is really my scene. It certainly had a feeling of playing "dress up." It was a bit surreal. Maybe that is OK. I was honored to be a part of the celebration to honor this man. It was an honor to be in this home of the U.S. embassy representative, to meet the movers and shakers. And yet…when the waiter I was talking to was dismissed and told he was no longer needed, and the gentleman who dismissed him said, "He doesn't know his place."—I was left to question mine as well. I was a caterer before, for a summer in Chicago. I know what it is like to be on the other side of this social play we were acting out. I had started the conversation with the waiter—was it my fault? I went to the party feeling privileged to attend, and left there wondering about the privilege granted to some, but not all of us. I could chalk that night up to experience. But what of the waiter—what was his "experience?" As I looked out over the rooftop deck of this apartment in the most coveted area of Rome, I pondered again the difference between the "haves" and the "have nots."

Thank you, Mr. Fulbright, for this opportunity. Thank you again for the chance to come to Italy and live and study and learn—I will be eternally grateful. Thank you also for allowing me a chance to see what "the other side of the fence" is like. I truly appreciate it. Am I privileged? Absolutely, I am privileged, in many ways. Yet when I left that party I had a very real sense of "now I will go back to my side, where I belong."

4

My Real Life Experiences with Italian Bureaucracy

You may have heard the stories, the rumors, and the negative stereotypes of the Italian government. If not, let me fill you in. If you have heard, then here are just some more examples to reinforce your already awful impression of the Italian system…

Italian bureaucracy at its finest

Lest you get the idea from me that Italy is all beauty and charm, let me tell you a story…Today I spent the entire morning at the police station. I have been trying to obtain my "permisso di sorrgornio"—it is like a residency permit to live here. I thought that I was fully prepared. I had made copies of all of the documents they needed, everything listed as requirements for this permit. Obtaining these things was no small feat either. It required: 1) a trip to the U.S. embassy for verification of my passport, 2) a visit to the Fulbright office for a letter of confirmation, 3) walking excursions to 9 different "tabbachi" shops, in order to find one that sold the right stamp that I needed to purchase, 4) a jaunt to a photo place to have 6 passport photos made, 5) a visit to the apartment rental agency to get a letter of verification of residence (honestly, I can't take credit for that, my roommate got it for me, but still, it had to be done), and 6) a return trip to the Fulbright office for verification materials of my medical insurance. The police station needed copies of every page of my passport that has a stamp on it, as well as the phone number of my sponsor here so that they could call and verify that all these forms that I had already made trips to collect where in fact "valid." I had the appropriate signatures, which were on official letterhead, and were exactly what was asked for. All of these materials were photocopied and collated into 4 sets.

When I went to the station today, I had the attitude of, "OK, I have done all that they asked. I have been very thorough and careful in following the rules. I know that others have had difficulty with this process, but I think I crossed all the t's and dotted all of the i's and I am going in there with a positive attitude." Well, it took about 5 seconds before that was shot down. As I approached the gentleman at the desk and indicated that, "I would like to obtain my "permisso di sorrgornio"...He just shook his head. "No." I had not yet had a chance to show him all of my carefully attained documents, and he was saying, "C'e` impossible`" which means "it is impossible." He leafed through these papers that I had carefully organized, not reading any of them. He found the one he was looking for—the letter from the landlady of my apartment, which served as my proof that I had a place to live and would not be relying on the Italian government for support. He said he needed the original, not a photocopy. I carefully, without wanting to be perceived as obnoxious or in anyway disrespectful. *(I have had incidents with the Italian police in the past, if you will remember, and I was not going to do anything to make this man angry with me.)* I pulled out the next paper in the stack, which was a photocopy of a postcard I had received from this very police station, indicating that they had received the original document. I thought for sure—"Here is my proof! You have it in your possession." This man was unimpressed with my letter. He indicated that the paper in question resided on the 3rd floor, while he works on the 1st floor. No brainer, right? I offered to walk up to the 3rd floor and retrieve the document for him, saying that I could be back in a few moments. The man motioned to the security guard, who was holding a very large, machine-type gun in his hand, to block the pathway up the stairs. OK—guess I would not be trying that approach....

The man behind the counter motioned for me to come closer, as if he were going to whisper something to me. When I was so close that I could feel his breathing on my face and hear his whiskers moving back and forth on his turtleneck, he yelled at me. He did not want me to go and get the original paper, he wanted me to go and get the landlord so that he could witness her signing this form. He made it quite clear that I was taking his time and he did not appreciate it. Then he lit his cigarette, and sat and smoked it, while others waited in line for his service.

After a scene like that, what I wanted to do was run. But I still had too many questions.... Take for instance the fact that I was renting my apartment through an agency. I had never even met this woman that I was supposed to bring with me to sign the document in front of him. How could I do that? I doubted very much that she would be willing to accompany me in this endeavor, probably realizing that it would not be pleasant. What was I to do? Without a permissio di sor-rgornio, I could be deported, without notice or question. I had already been there a month and didn't yet have it. Technically, you are legally supposed to obtain this within your first week of residence. I don't honestly know how that could be possible to get it done in that much time, given all that is required, and the delays inherent in having to wait for agencies and people to write letters. I was standing outside the police station, a million ideas running through my head.

Whether out of self-dignity, stupidity, or lack of knowing what else to do (probably a bit of all three), I re-entered the police station. I decided to approach the first officer I had encountered, the only one that had smiled at me. I politely approached him to see if he would mind if I asked him a question. He simply said, "Certo" (Of course). I explained that I was not trying to be disrespectful, but I was not sure how I could get the landlady that I have never met, to join me at the police station. He nodded a sympathetic nod, smiled, and then looked at the "ruler" of the decisions and said, "It just depends on who is helping you out. Perhaps if you came back on a different day, it might be different," he said, still smiling. "In Italy, the rules are always changing…"

I, of course, thought to myself, "Or it might be exactly the same man, the same man who will of course remember me because he had to call the security guy on me so that I wouldn't go up the stairs. He will know that I am trying to "get away" with only having all the documents that I am supposed to have, but not having the lady to sign another original in his presence." Just then, I glanced over at the man with all the power, who was smoking a cigarette as the line inside his office grew longer and longer. I left the premises immediately, before he could see that I had come back.

I don't have a permit to live here, and I don't know how I will go about obtaining one. I just placed a call into the rental agency, so we'll see….

At the bank

So I walked into the bank, prepared for whatever might come my way—cops with machine guns, being yelled at by a security guard, or being told they just wouldn't cash my check (no reason necessary, they are the bank after all, and they can decide). My previous check-cashing experience was difficult, and resulted in two separate trips there, the second time with a letter from the Fulbright Commission stating that this was indeed a check issued by them and that I had their permission to cash it. This check was only a reimbursement check, for $100. A lot for me, but not much for that bank, so I had hoped that it would go smoother, but I wasn't counting on it. This is Italy—wait and see…

As I approached the cashier, I was surprised and delighted to see him smile at me. "OK, good start" I thought, "now use your best Italian and get this thing cashed!" We made small talk, first about me being a "borsa di studi" and then about my last name. He teased that my passport should be from Poland, not from America, and said he had never met an American with that last name. Of course I thought, "Most Americans haven't heard it either, and even fewer can spell it." He said he would just take my passport, make a photocopy, and then would be back with my money. Wow—piece of cake! Okay…going well.

When he returned, he handed me back my passport, and then asked me to go out with him. I looked at him, thinking, "Are you serious?" I was a bit surprised that he would be so forward at work. I said, "No, but thank you." He took my money, put it under the counter and walked around the office, lamely trying to look busy. This is his approach to dating? Holding random someone's money? Is this supposed to be a turn on? His co-workers witnessed this entire interaction; surely they would think it was harassment. Nope—they gave him "high fives." I stood at the counter, not knowing what to do. I couldn't jump over the counter and take the money, there is an armed security guard here too, and so, well—I am not completely stupid. Should I yell to the manager? No wait—he had "high-fived" the worker. Now that they have the check in their possession, I couldn't grab the check and go to another bank. I thought all these things, and I did nothing. Stood there. Waited. The cashier returned after an eternity (or about 5 minutes, depending on who you ask), and again asked for a date. "Maybe I could say, yes and then give him the wrong number," I thought. "Maybe if I say yes, he will hand the money over and then I can run…" Never mind, the security guard with the machine gun was now watching the whole incident. I decided that saying yes would be chickening out, so I again said, "No, I am sorry." The money remained under the counter and out of my reach. By now I was determined. I wouldn't leave without my money, and I wouldn't tell him that I would go on a date with him. I was standing my ground, thinking,"…but he has to be here anyway, since he is working. This really could take all day…"

Another eternity later (clock time was probably closer to 4 minutes), after pretending to look at the inside of the copy machine, making coffee, and opening some envelopes on another person's desk, the cashier returned. He looked at me, questioning with his eyebrows raised, as if to say, "Well, are you ready to give in?" I responded with a gesture too…no, not that one, but I wanted to. I slowly shook my head from side to side. I wasn't giving in. Defeated, he handed me the money and then glared. So much for having a "pleasant experience" in one of Italian's public office buildings.

I still have to go back for that "permisso di sorrgornio" thing...can't wait.

Another encounter with the cops

Now, most people would call me a "good girl," really. I have to make that clear to those of you reading this and interpreting my run-ins with the police as an indication of my character. I am honest—I have a hard time lying and I am bad at it. I see my purpose in life as helping others, and doing as little harm as possible to those things and beings around me. Sure, I like to have fun, but seriously, I am not what you might call a "trouble maker." You can even ask my parents, they would tell you I wasn't a bad kid, not too hard to raise, like...oh, I don't know...say, for example...my brothers.

Having said that let me tell you about what happened this weekend with the police. I was walking across the main Piazza in Bologna, when a man approached me. He was walking directly toward me, very quickly. He was unkempt and disheveled looking, and I assumed he would be asking me for money. He continued walking directly toward me, looking at me, never looking away. His gaze was penetrating and scary. I stepped to the side in an effort to let him pass. He didn't pass, but shifted in the same direction, without moving his eyes. He got closer and closer, until he was very close to me, maybe 3 inches from my face. He told me he needed money, and that he hadn't eaten in days. He pushed my shoulder and demanded that I give him my bag. He was spitting on me as he yelled his request. I told shook my head "No." *This man was frightening, and I have no intention of opening my bag in front of him, or of giving him anything.*

I had my bag over my shoulder, and I grasped it tighter. He was not backing down. *Surely he won't do anything with all these people watching...Just as quickly as that thought popped into my brain, I thought of the social psychology class that I had taught on the "bystander effect"—that a large group of people is less likely to respond to such an event because they assume someone else will.* It is ironic how time can pass so slowly in moments like that, when you can contemplate the most rational things, and you feel afraid at the same time.

The man reached for my bag and attempted to take it from me. He cursed me and told me I would "pay" for not cooperating. I had been ready though, because I knew when he first approached me that he might attempt such a thing. I held the strap of my bag with my left hand, and punched the man in the abdomen with my right. He hunched over, holding his stomach. I stepped back, a bit stunned from what had just transpired, and noted a carabinari approaching me. *Good, he can arrest this man for trying to attack me!* Except that he didn't. The policeman saw me punch this man, and wanted to question me as to why I was disturbing the peace. "What? Are you kidding? He tried to take my bag!" I said. "He is a homeless man, and weak. He would not try to steal from you," replied the policeman.

I was angry and confused. The man stood up and walked away without even being questioned. I saw him round the corner of the church, and then the carabinari said, "I will need to see your documents." I would never see that man again, and he would never be talked to about his attempt to steal my things. I was frustrated that I would be questioned. I was shaking a bit from the episode, and felt sick. *What did I have to gain from punching a guy? What did this police think I was—crazy? I am not going to go up to someone on the street and punch him! I was surprised it happened even when it did. Oh my goodness—I really punched a guy and kept him from stealing my purse!* At that moment, as the carabinari was looking at each and every page of my passport, and asking me why I had gone to Germany and in what month I had visited England. *I am so thankful for having brothers that wrestled with me and "played tough" so that I could take this guy (granted he was tiny and hungry, but still), and I am thankful for Tae Bo (Billy Blanks would have been proud of how I put my weight into that punch!).*

"What?" I asked. "I said, what month did you travel to England," he replied. *Oh my goodness—back to the questions about me. I don't remember, I went to England—6 or was it 8 years ago? Let's see…I think it was spring break time.* "Perhaps it was in March." "And the dates?" he asked. *Does he think I really remember that? This cop won't ask a single question of the man who tried to steal my bag, but he is asking me about the dates I spent in England I don't know how many years ago?*

"I think it was mid-March, around the week of the 20th." "Are you sure?" he asked. *NO, I am guessing here. Why do you care???* "I cannot be sure, since it was several years ago, but I believe I went in the spring." "OK." *NOW are you going to chase that guy or something?*

"You are an American?" *If I weren't afraid of the Italian police, I would tell you how dumb of a question that is, given that my passport is in your hand, which clearly states that I am and you have been fondling it for minutes.* "Yes, I am," I say. The policeman asked, "How long are you staying in Italy?" *OH NO—I see where this is going. I could lie and say I am visiting for 2 weeks, but (as I have already mentioned) I really suck at lying, and can never pull it off. Here goes…*"I am living in Rome, I am a student here on a scholarship for 4 months," I replied. "Please let me see your permisso di sorggornio." *OK, I really don't believe this.* I told him the story. He was unimpressed that I have been in Italy so long without being "legal." After several minutes that felt like hours, with my heart in my throat—fears of being deported running through my mind—and anger in my stomach that I couldn't release because that would have led to more trouble for me. In the end, the policeman told me repeatedly how nice he was for letting me go "this time" *if you were really nice, you would have done something about the purse thief…*"Yes, sir. Thank you."

I know people who have lived abroad for years and never been asked about their residency permit. I have met a person here who never knew she was supposed to have one, and she has been in Rome for a year. Some folks don't bother; they think no one will ever know. What are the chances that you could really be stopped by a policeman and asked for your documents in just a 4-month period? What are the chances it could happen to the same person so many times? When you are me—the odds seem to change.

Then again, I still had my purse, my passport, everything I had brought with me—and I had punched the guy who tried to take them. So it all depends on how you look at it, I guess. I decided to appreciate what had happened. Admittedly it took a couple hours to get to the point where I could do that—my pulse needed to return to normal and I needed some alone time to think it all through. In the end, I decided it makes for a more interesting story than "I was walking across the piazza and it was totally normal. Nothing happened."

Another Encounter at the Bank

I went to the bank today. Yep, you guessed it, another bank story. The bank was closed. It was 11am, and the opening hours are from 9am-1pm, then again from 2:45-4:00 p.m. I rang the buzzer to be let in, to no avail. I rang it again, thinking it must be broken or something, since no one answered. At the third ring, the security guard came over to me and told me the bank was closed and that I should go. "Why?" I asked. "Because," he replied. I asked if they would open later in the day. "No. We are closed today." I searched for a sign on the day indicating it was a holiday—nothing. No reason given. The security guard seemed annoyed that I would even ask why the bank was not open, as if his word should have been enough. He locked the door behind him, and motioned me to "shoo away." Have I mentioned how much I like going to the bank in Italy?

My latest encounter with the Italian police—
My thoughts on this experience

Marianna, my research assistant, is driving. She says, "The police behind us have their lights flashing, that is just like America" (they usually wave a red baton out the window to pull people over in Italy).

I say, "That means you have to pull over." *Haven't you at least seen the movies?*

"No, I don't think so, I have never seen that in Italy before."

"I really think you should pull over, if they don't want you, they will keep going." *I wonder why they could be pulling us over? We weren't speeding, haven't been drinking, and obeyed all of the signs. Humm.*

"This can't be happening. It must be because you are with me. You have trouble with the police, don't you?" *You have to bring that up now? You are right—I hope they don't ask for my permisso—I still don't have it, and probably never will get it. Shit.*

"Yes. That is why maybe you should pull over, it is will be more trouble with the police if they think you are not obeying." *Now would be a good time. Really.*

Reluctantly, Marianna turns the corner, and says, "They do want me! Oh mio Dio. Now what do I do?" *You wait for them to walk up and tell you why they pulled you over. This really has never happened to you before?*

"Try stopping. They will want to walk up here and talk to you."

"This only happens in America, never in Italy!" she says. *You are with me. This really can happen.*

The policemen approached, and asked Marianna why she did not pull over sooner. "I didn't know what to do," she says. "I thought that was only in America where they turned on the lights and chased you down."

"Haven't you seen the movies, don't you know you should stop?" *Act cool, they won't know I am American if they just talk to her and don't look at me.*

Marianna is laughing, "I didn't do anything wrong, I was even wearing my seatbelt, and I don't always do that." *Oh mio Dio is right! Why would she tell him that? Clearly, I have had more experience with this than she is has. Great.*

The policeman looks at me, "You are American, right? You don't look Italian. Your eyes are blue. I will need to see your documents." *OK—I don't have my passport with me, only my driver's license. I will act confident and hand that to him, and hope he looks at it briefly and then lets us go.*

"Here you go."

"Your other documents. I need to see your passport and your permisso di sorggornio." *They always say to not carry your passport with you because you don't want to lose it. OK—how do I get myself out of this one? I can't run—he has a gun. That would be a bad idea. This sucks. I guess I will go with honesty and hope that gets me somewhere.*

"My passport is at my home. I have applied for my permisso di sorggornio, but I don't have it yet." *Of course, I am saying all of this in Italian, and hoping it is clear to him. He is looking at me like I am a freak. Stop that!*

"Which questura did you use to apply for the permisso? I will put in a call to them and see." *Oh great. He calls them, they tell him they don't have it, then what? I applied, but they didn't accept my application.* "Haven't you seen the movies, don't you know you should stop?" *Act cool, they won't know I am American if they just talk to her and don't look at me.*

Marianna is laughing, "I didn't do anything wrong, I was even wearing my seat-belt, and I don't always do that." *Oh mio Dio is right! Why would she tell him that? Clearly, I have had more experience with this than she is has. Great.*

The policeman looks at me, "You are American, right? You don't look Italian. Your eyes are blue. I will need to see your documents." *OK—I don't have my passport with me, only my driver's license. I will act confident and hand that to him, and hope he looks at it briefly and then lets us go.*

"Here you go."

"Your other documents. I need to see your passport and your permisso di sorggornio." *They always say to not carry your passport with you because you don't want to lose it. OK—how do I get myself out of this one? I can't run—he has a gun. That would be a bad idea. This sucks. I guess I will go with honesty and hope that gets me somewhere.*

"My passport is at my home. I have applied for my permisso di sorggornio, but I don't have it yet." *Of course, I am saying all of this in Italian, and hoping it is clear to him. He is looking at me like I am a freak. Stop that!*

"Which questura did you use to apply for the permisso? I will put in a call to them and see." *Oh great. He calls them, they tell him they don't have it, then what? I applied, but they didn't accept my application. I have*

I give him the address I think is on the card, except that address is on the sticker on the back, since I have moved. This is clearly very confusing to him. "Don't you know where you live? Are you lying?" With that comment, he puts his hand on his gun. *OK—let's see that address on the front was from when I first moved to Maryland…let's see…I have lived in 2 other places since then…*"OK…I know it…"

"What is this number?"

"That is the driver's license number."

"That must be very important. What is your number?" *I have no idea. I have never, ever learned my driver's license number. I know in some states it is the social security number, but I know mine is not. It starts with S...crap.*

"I know that it starts with "S"—I don't know the other numbers. We never use that number in the States."

"Then why is it on your card?" *Humm—I don't think he believes me. But—he seemed angry before, but now he seems to be enjoying toying with me. Maybe I can redirect him. It is worth a shot.*

"Why did you say you pulled us over?"

"Just like an American to question authority!" *He is smiling. OK—go with it.*

"Well, it seems like if we were doing something wrong you would want to tell us so that we could correct it." *Polite, "innocent," I think he is going for it—but I also think I am making my point. Why did he pull us over, anyway?*

"We are "controlling." We pick a car and pull them over to see if everything is OK, make sure everyone is legal." He says, and then winks at me.

"Oh I see, that is very important. Why did you pick us?" *Don't you have crimes to solve? Murderers to catch? People actually breaking the law that you need to ticket or something? There is always that mafia thing you could work on if you are getting bored.*

"Two girls in a car laughing as you passed us. Why not?" *He is actually saying that he picked our car because he could tell there were 2 women in the car? Oh my...*

"So we didn't break any laws? We are free to go?" *Maybe he has forgotten about the permisso...I can hope.*

"Well, I would let you go but you are not here legally." *His memory is better than I had hoped. Crap. Now what?*

Marianna pipes in, "I have all the documents you need for the car. That is why you stopped us anyway, right? To be sure we had it registered and had insurance? You wouldn't stop us just because we were two women, now would you?" *OK—way to jump in there. Let's hope he goes for it.*

Marianna tells him, "The car is registered in my father's name, and it is our family vehicle. Here is his information, on this card." *She is a genius! Her father works for the Italian government. He is kind of a big wig. His documents show that. Yes!*

The policeman says, "Thank you, miss, for showing us those. You are free to go." *You are kidding? That is it? Nothing else? No jail for me, at least not for tonight! Wow. That was surreal. OK—breathe normal.*

And Marianna drove me home.

5

Discovering Places

Italy is gorgeous, romantic, wonderful, and breathtaking. In my effort to live in the moment, I spent most weekends away from Rome, exploring the country. I was repeatedly struck by the uniqueness and beauty that surrounded me. Although a picture can paint a thousand words, a thousand words cannot paint an accurate picture for you of this land. I know this, but let me try...

Ostia Antica

At the suggestion of a friend, I visited Ostia Antica—the former port city of Rome, which was the port until the Tiber river changed course and the entire Roman empire was altered. This place was not even mentioned in my guidebook to Italy, though I have seen it listed elsewhere as "The prettier Pompeii." It was amazingly beautiful. I spent an entire day exploring the ruins that comprised a city that lasted for over 2000 years. This port town is triangulated by the sea, the river, and some mountains. Today, the "Antica" part only exists in the form of ruins and a museum, though Ostia itself was rebuilt so that it would remain along the river. I saw the oldest existing house with a roof, and one of the oldest known temples built to all of the gods, before Christianity arrived in Italy. The layout of the city is well preserved—and one can imagine the workings of the bakers, the grocers, and the city council elders.

Given its location, water was of great importance to the inhabitants of Ostia Antica. Their many fountains were decorated as fish and depicted the vastness and bounty of the sea around them. They made tiles that covered the floors of the public baths and they were quite artistic in this endeavor. The city seemed to celebrate the athletes among them, dedicating many floors to competitions such as wrestling and discus throwing.

There was a particular set of tiles—in the deepest of the baths, dedicated to "individual water gymnastics." I loved that! The art looked as though people were moving underwater with their noses plugged. I pictured the people that lived there 3000 years ago, doing somersaults in the water and holding their breathe—trying to see who could do the most rotations before having to come up for air. Or how about walking on one's hands with the legs out of the water? I left there with a sense of, "They were just like me!!" How many times did I do that as a child? Or for that matter, how many times did I do that the last time I went swimming? It seems we are the same—spanning centuries and continents....

Why do we focus on the differences among us?

Assisi—The City of Peace

I spent this weekend in Assisi, a beautiful small town situated half-way up a mountain, with gorgeous views below of the valley and rolling hills, and the vistas of snow-covered mountains above. The city has retained its charm and friendliness, despite the fact that it receives many tourists each year. I walked the town in its entirety a few times, at first getting my bearings and exploring what was there, and then going back to see the things I had missed the first time; to explore the smaller streets, the *viale* and the *viccolas*, and to get a better sense of "place" rather than "sights." The penetrating cold wind prevented the many tourists from exploring, and the streets were vacant, except for the shopkeepers that came out to talk amongst themselves and the local people who were out to grab a bite to eat. I felt privileged to visit this wonderful place, so often visited before, and to feel as though I was not a "visitor" at all, but a welcome friend in this city of peace.

St. Francis—what a guy! For those of you who know much more about this topic, please forgive my ignorance and any errors that I might make in reporting the "facts" of his life. My knowledge of St. Francis, prior to this trip, was that he was the saint of the animals. I could recall a hymn that I had been taught in elementary school, about St. Francis saving the animals and I had seen pictures of him walking in his "monk" outfit, with his arm outstretched for a bird to land on his hand. That was about all I knew. But here is some of what I learned:

St. Francis was born to well-to-do parents that lived in the town of Assisi. He had many privileges because of this money, and was raised to be a "good citizen." In his early years (around 20 years of age), he denounced his father's wealth and decided to live a life of poverty. It is reported that St. Francis "heard a voice from on high" that he should change the Catholic church, because it was full of greed. He challenged the church to change its ways. This was no small feat for a young man living in a time when the papacy *was* the state, and Francis was imprisoned for taking this position. (Italy didn't declare separation of church and state until 1984, and even now there is debate about that). People who challenged the Catholic church during this time were frequently killed for being heretics. Speaking out against the evils of some of the popes, announcing the blatant manner in which they disobeyed their own laws (I read that, until the 18th century, 80% of the popes bore children out of wedlock), and encouraging others to disobey this almighty force took courage in the true sense of the word. St. Francis stood up for what he really believed in, and he made a difference. Amazing.

By obtaining the backing of a few church officials, he was set free from jail, and was allowed to practice his teachings, which were mainly those of peace and brotherhood, as well as the creed that all people were created equal (including woman and people of various colors, which predates our constitutional interpretation of "all are created equal" by about 800 years). St. Catherine believed as Francis did, and left her family and fortunes, to live a life of poverty and service. Separately, Francis and Catherine founded the first organized places where people of faith could live together in worship and service. It is believed that the first orphanage was located in Assisi to take care of the sick. The service works of the followers of these two continues today, not only in this town, but in the way that the Catholic church later adopted some of these practices, whereby nuns, priests, monks, and other "people of the cloth" provided services to those in need.

You know what else I like about Francis? He wrote about the wind. Not only animals, but also of the forces of nature. His canticle to the wind is inspiring. The wind has long been my favorite force of nature. It is not visible, except in the actions that it causes and the movement it creates. Wind is powerful, it can knock down buildings and change the course of rivers, yet it can be as subtle as the gentle breeze on your face that allows you to know the smell of the area surrounding you—the ocean, the trees, and the flowers. I love to walk in the breeze, to feel its presence surrounding my body, enveloping me. The wind reminds me that I am not alone in a sea of humanity; it goes between and amongst us and connects us all.

On climbing a mountain

Having just spent the previous day talking about the events of the world and seeing all of the sights in the city of Assisi, I set out on Sunday morning without a plan. I was feeling reflective and thoughtful and wanted to appreciate as much of my surroundings as possible, before leaving to go back to the city. I went to the

Foro Romano, and saw the evidence of the Roman Empire in Assisi. Next I went to the Pinoteca, and saw works of art by Assisians, the famous and non-famous alike. I was particularly struck by one painting there, of "St. Giacomo after he murdered his parents." I don't know the story behind that one at all, but the picture was a bloody painting among the many beautiful ones of Madonna & Child. He was a saint who killed his parents. I like St. Francis better. I wondered the edge of the town and climbed the towers, and took a lot of pictures. At one end of town, I saw a small trail that I thought would take me out over the edge of that particular hill and grant me a gorgeous view of the town. I hiked the trail to the edge of the hill and saw the view and noted that the trail kept going, and so I followed it. I did not know where the trail would lead, except that I knew it was going up. Maybe to those mountains I could see with snow on the top? Maybe to some place gorgeous and mysterious? Maybe….

I followed the trail up—straight up. I continued walking and enjoying the view, and then the hiking became more challenging. It truly was straight up, without a cutback in sight. I could feel the blood pumping in my thighs, and hear my heart pounding in my ears. I began to feel warm, despite the cold winds that had kept me bundled previously, with my scarf over my face and my gloves on my hands. I wondered, "How long is this trail? Where will it take me?" I wondered for some time, and then got lost in the nature around me.

This was amazing! I saw birds that I had never seen before, and their chirps were unlike anything I remember hearing. I saw an animal on the trail—maybe a fox? Maybe something else, but I couldn't make it out. I thought, "I am in a different country, on a different continent. It is entirely possible that there are animals here that I have never seen!" What an amazing feeling that was! It was like exploring and discovering a new world. Yet, the trees looked much like those in Maryland, and the rocks—well, I am no geologist, but they looked like normal rocks to me, except that I could see some marble, and the colors looked lighter to me, though it was difficult to tell, because by now I had reached the height where the ground was covered with snow. Interesting, how the trees looked so much like those in Maryland, and so different from the Oregon trees where I grew up. This interesting contradiction was not lost on me on that day.

I continued walking, and began to question the wisdom of it. I had some water with me, but no food. I was wearing black boots, not my hiking boots, but my "all around boots"—which were better than dress shoes, but not by much. I was also wearing slacks, the same ones I had worn out the evening before for dinner on the town. I was traveling light; I had only brought my daypack with me, for my weekend stay in Assisi. I had no "wicking clothes" and was wearing cotton—not good for an occasion when one might sweat, and then have that sweat freeze to your body. I contemplated all these things, and continued anyway. Why should I climb this mountain? Because it was there. Because it needed to be climbed. Because I needed to climb a mountain that day. And so I did.

The views from the top were amazing. The landscape was snow-covered, sunny, windy, and beautiful. I reflected on friends who had helped me to get here, those currently "in my life" and those that have been a part of it in the past. I thought about the blessings I have received, the fortunes that have come my way, and the challenges that I faced in order to be where I was at the moment. I would not have been at the top of that mountain without each of them, and for each I felt grateful. I walked down the mountain, singing to myself, and enjoying the view. It had definitely been worth the walk. Climbing a mountain doesn't seem like that big of a deal, if you *just take it one step at a time*. It also helps if you are unaware of how high, steep and long the trail is. You just keep going and you will get there, eventually.

The coliseum

I finally made it inside. I live near it, see it regularly, run around its perimeter, and marvel at its grandeur, despite its decline. I was saving the visit inside to do with a guest. It was neat. I have seen movies that showed the coliseum, and PBS specials that talked about the history and design of the monument. All of those things helped me to better appreciate it. However, the sense of being in that place, and imagining the events that occurred there was remarkable. I could see where the emperors had sat, had given the "thumbs up" to save a gladiators life, or had done the reverse. I saw the intricate maze that would have been under the floor of the coliseum, which held the animals until they were charged to battle. I could see the "elevators" that the workers had used to cart the slaves up to the stadium to face their potential death.

The women and children in attendance were required to sit near the top. I wondered what a child thought when he saw a man murdered by another? This was sport. Maybe it didn't seem real? Maybe the slaves were "them" and not "us" which allowed the children (and adults) to separate themselves enough to not think that killing for sport was a bad idea. Interesting—don't we still do that now? Right now, it seems the "them" are Arab, or Muslim, or Middle Eastern. If they aren't like us, we can distance ourselves. Killing is OK as long as God is on *our side*, right? The Romans thought so....

I thought about the show of power that was the coliseum. They used animals from Africa, that were exotic and from a land far away, to show that this land, too, had been "conquered." I wondered about the cost of attendance at this cultural show of "see and be seen." How likely was a peasant farmer to attend a fight of the gladiators? Labeled as the "physical evidence of Roman power"—I wondered how the regular folks, the populace, perceived these events? As the Roman empire diminished, was it difficult to get people to come to the coliseum? Did it then become a "poor man's sport" after the rich were no longer interested? After the coliseum ceased to be used as a public building, it fell into decline. The beams were taken from it, and melted down for the metal. Marble was pilfered. Now, it is again perceived as grand.

It is amazing. The coliseum is beautiful and in ruin. It portrays power and vulnerability. One cannot help but wonder what the world was like "back then." I know that it is not possible to interpret history using today's ethics. Yet one can wonder....

"My Bologna has a first name, it's..."

I spent the weekend in Bologna! That's right, of Oscar Meyer fame. Well, this bologna came first, but it is still famous for its meat. I never liked the stuff myself, and haven't eaten it in years (since the days of school lunches, fake cheese, white bread, and miracle whip). Yet, it was great to visit this interesting city in the Emelio-Reggio region of Italy.

Bologna hosts the oldest continuously running university in the Western world, dating from 1088. It has the definite feel of a university town, and I liked it very much. As a major university for classical studies and literature, it draws people from around the globe. There were people of various colors, backgrounds, ethnicities, beliefs, and religions. It was wonderful to be around such an interesting mix of people. Speaking generally here, university towns tend to celebrate such diversity and draw interesting people to it. I have to couch that in specific terms, since my time in Kentucky was spent in a university town that bordered several "dry towns"—so I tend to believe the meaning of "university towns" is not nation-wide! People in Kentucky did not congregate for the cultural activities as much as they did for the Thursday night/Ladies night at the bars in town. But I digress...

The piazza was a gathering place on Sunday for families, school-age children playing games, and a group from Cuba playing music that included the pan flute (and you KNOW they played the Titanic theme song). There were groups of

African teenagers playing bongos and dancing, young adults demonstrating their love all over the place, and a heavy metal electric guitar player, with a motorcycle, not a motorino (and folks did not know what to make of that!). Although it was not a particular day of celebrations (it wasn't a Saint Day, at least that I know of), there were people out celebrating this and that, and hosting tables for various causes. I signed a petition to help the student environmental action team get better buses to reduce the impact of smog on the city. It was a beautiful day. It is difficult to describe how different Bologna feels from Rome. It was nice, quiet, interesting, and happening all at the same time.

The sidewalks in Bologna are all covered, creating a sense of involvement in the city. Everywhere there are grand archways, and overhead there are magnificent buildings that have withstood the test of time. In the center, the roads are much too narrow for cars, so people walk. This closeness provides a sense of community that I really enjoy. Upon entering the city, I walked the length of a street covered with fruit vendors, carrying the most gorgeous fruit I have seen. I bought my first strawberries of the season and made my way to a park to have a seat on the bench, eat my lunch of fruit and more fruit, and people watch. The sun was out, my jacket was off, and I was completely content to be away for the weekend and exploring this new place, even if I did not intend to eat any bologna.

The Vatican and the Sistine Chapel

I had been to the Vatican before, on my previous one-week tour of Italy. At that time, my aunt Linda (known ever since that trip as "Zia"—meaning aunt in Italian) spent a couple of days in Rome before going to the beautiful Amalfi coast. We saw the Vatican and the Pope. This time, though, it felt different to me. I had time to take it all in.

We joined an English-speaking group with a young, hip, and very funny tour guide. I learned more about the important artwork on the walls, the ceiling, and the dome. One artist was commissioned to create some art for a dying pope, which was not to be revealed until the pope died. At the ceremony commemorating the statue, a huge crowd was gathered to witness this new art in honor of their Papa`. The artist, being a Protestant, apparently didn't like the whole Pope thing; because when they uncovered the artwork, it was not the Popes face that they saw, but that of the young artist. How scandalous! I wouldn't have known that just walking around on my own. I learned that Michelangelo signed his famous work of Mary holding Christ after he was removed from the cross (known as Pieta`), because he was from Florence, and the Roman artists didn't think such a work was possible coming from a place so far away as Florence (it is about 1 ½ hours away by train, these days). I learned that the Tomb of St. Peter is kept in the basement of the Vatican—also known as St. Peter's Basilica. There has been speculation for years as to whether the relics actually belonged to the original St. Peter. Seems that carbon dating that has happened in the last few years indicate that the bones really are old enough to have come from that era. And the feet bones are missing…the story goes that Peter was hung on a cross upside down, and when he was taken off; his followers cut him down at the ankles, leaving his feet behind. Humm…

The Vatican is beautiful. It is amazing. It is grand and huge. It houses works of art, and is a work of art in and of itself. The dome, the highest in the city, can be seen from many vantage points throughout Rome. The Vatican demands respect, yet it is playful and hints at the fun of the personalities of those involved in its construction. Though Michelangelo built the tallest dome in town, it is not the widest—the widest dome belongs to the Pantheon. He intentionally kept his dome narrower, as was articulated to his fellow builders. He did this out of respect for the artists that came before him. I like that.

And then there were the Vatican Museums. Our guide told us that if you spent 60 seconds looking at each piece of art in the Vatican Museums, you would be there for 12 years. That is without bathroom breaks! So—Caroline and I didn't do the whole thing. We did see the work by Rafael (amazing!!), especially his *School of Athens* painting—which made me feel as though I was with all those people, walking through the city street, contemplating with them the topics of human thought and knowledge. It was truly great work by an amazing artist. It was so amazing to feel "in the presence" of someone that passed 500 years before I was born.

The Sistine Chapel—wow! Most people know of *The Creation of Adam*, by Michelangelo, or at least would probably recognize it if shown a picture. Before visiting here, I had thought that painting was alone on the ceiling, without realizing that the entire ceiling, in fact the entire room of the Sistine Chapel, is covered by amazing paintings and artwork. *The Last Judgment,* also my Michelangelo, covers the wall behind the alter from floor to ceiling, and depicts 300 figures in various states—from the damned souls and those rising to heaven. It is remarkable, gorgeous, and moving. This chapel is still used as a conclave—it is closed to the public upon the death of a pope, and it is the meeting place where the cardinals and other church officials meet to decide who will be the next pope, the leader of the Catholic church.

The power of the touch

There is this statue in the Vatican, dating from the 12th century. I don't recall who created it or what it represents, except that it was some saint, and the story goes that if you rubbed the foot of the saint, you would be blessed. People have been doing this for years and years. Now, the foot has become a stump. All the toes are gone from the touching. The church has officially now declared that if you rub the other foot, it will bring you blessings as well, trying to encourage people from touching what remains of the foot.

It is amazing, really, to think of the power of the touch. People are not rubbing the foot, just touching it. No one has sanded it away, and no damage has ever been reported to the statue. Through all these years, it has just worn away. The rest of the figure remains intact, without damage. I was struck by the power of the touch. We don't tend to think of our impact in that way, but what—and who—we touch, has a profound impact. Many touches put together...well...

The Baths of Caracalla

They are on the outskirts of Rome, though they are less well traveled than most of the sites in this city. At one time, the baths greeted 5000 visitors everyday. It housed tubs with water of different temperatures, heated floors so that your tootsies wouldn't be cold, and glass walkways going from one to the other, protecting you from the wind. The ruins that remain are impressive. In addition to the baths there were gymnasiums and exercise studios. There are many tile floors still visible, which lends a sense of wonder about the lives of those who came here before. How did it compare to gyms of today? Did they do "aerobic" activity? Did they really look as good as they do in all those statues?

Catacombs of San Callisto

The catacombs were built by the early Christians, when they were being persecuted because of their convictions. They buried their dead in catacombs, holding funerals underground, as well as church services, right next to the bodies of those who had died. The catacomb complex that we entered had four floors of burials, and covered 15 acres. The tour only led to the 2nd level, and the area we saw was much smaller, though one could still get a pretty good idea of what it might have felt like to be in a tunnel, hiding and practicing one's religion. The caverns for the bodies were quite small, both because the people living in those days were much shorter, and because they buried a lot of children. There were also family tombs, where an entire family could be buried together.

The first eight popes were buried in the catacomb that we entered. Their remains are now housed at the basilica near my home. Saint Cecilia, the patron saint of music, was buried in this catacomb as well. The art in the caves, as well as the tomb of St. Cecilia, depicts the figures holding up three fingers on one hand, one on the other—the demonstrate their belief in one god, three forms—the father, son, and holy ghost.

It was not as eerie as I thought it might be in the catacomb, though I imagine that with rotting bodies in there, it was a different experience entirely. It would be scary to get lost in there, wondering how to get out, and seeing more death in front of you at every turn.

The last comment made by the guide before we left, was that the average life span in those days was 32 years old. Wow. I think of myself as young, but according to those standards—yikes! We make decision these days that would never have been possible then, such as postponing having families, going to school until you are 30, not "settling down" until mid-life—also known as mid—to late—40s. We think of adolescence now as continuing into the early 20s, and don't think a person is old unless they act like it, or they are over 80. Thinking about that made me feel lucky that I live in a time when I potentially have the opportunity to do so many different things in my life. At the same time, we don't know that we will live that long. How might I live differently if I would not likely live longer than a few more years?

Florence—revisited

I spent a week in Florence in December, studying Italian at a school there. I returned in April after having lived in Rome for a few months…

It was interesting to feel a sense of "ownership" of this place. I did not need a map. I knew exactly how to get to the Duomo, to the Ponte Vecchio, the Piazza Signoria, the Uffici Gallery, and the marketplace. I knew the bridge to cross to get to the Palazzo Pitti and to go to the lesser-traveled parts of the city. It was a gorgeous day, and I had just been traveling in a train for over 6 hours. I needed to get out and walk around.

Although I had been in the Duomo and climbed to the top of it's huge dome, I had not been to the Baptistery, and so I went inside. I had seen the statue of David on my last trip there, but the buildings at the Palazzo Vecchio had been closed for restoration when I was there before, so this time I looked. It was the same, yet different. In December, it rained during the entire duration of my stay in Florence. On this day, it was gorgeous. The lights celebrating Natale (Christmas) that had just been placed when I first arrived in Florence were now replaced with store windows decorated for the coming of Pasque (Easter), an event in Italy whose importance supercedes that of Christmas. There were few tourists here the first time around, a drastic comparison to the hoards of people taking pictures simultaneously from different angles outside of the duomo. They have the right idea—it is picture worthy—interesting "layered" look of white, green, and pink marble.

It was in Florence that my Italian skills seemed to come together for the first time. I had studied the language in Sienna and learned a lot, but when I came to Florence, the things that I had learned began to take shape in my mind. It was here that I had my first "conversation" in Italian with a person that did not speak English, and was not another student struggling through the process of remembering vocabulary words so that we could piece together sentences. I had been in awe of the art that was readily available on every street, on each building, in all of the galleries and museums. Those things were still there, and they were still beautiful, though I didn't feel in awe—I felt comfortable.

I approached the venders, who had previously scared me a bit with their bargaining tactics, and felt confident. In speaking with a vendor in Italian, I was able to make my point, to walk away when I wanted to, and to "play the game" with them, instead of having it played on me. It became fun…and I have a new leather jacket to show for my time there.

I was glad to have returned to Florence. It served as a good reminder for me as to how far I had come—not only in my language skills and in living abroad—but also in how this experience has changed my perspective on things. I handle myself differently, and feel more confident. I am less weary of new experiences; I tend to embrace them because I learn from each and every one of them. I have grown in my ability to "tumble with the punches" and make the most out of situations that I would not have asked for. I didn't make it to Reggio Emelia that day, which had been frustrating to me—but I did see Florence in a whole new light. What might, in a previous time, have made me mad, led me to feel down on myself, or ruined my whole day, instead turned into an opportunity to see the changes that have occurred in me. That is a powerful thing, I realized as I sat in the Palazzo, sipping a café in the Mediterranean sunshine.

Pescara—city by the sea

Pescara is unlike any other Italian city that I have visited. It is not old. It does not have ruins. There are no old buildings of stone, no ancient walls or aqueducts. This city was bombed out completely during WWII by the Germans. It has since been rebuilt, mostly in 1950s style architecture. What was once a maritime force to be reckoned with, is now a thriving beach town, focusing on fishing and the small tourist business it draws, mostly Romanian, Polish, and German tourists. The Italians tend to stay at the beaches on the West coast. The beaches were clear and clean, and the beach umbrellas were being set up for the summer season. The town is walk able. It has its fair share of car traffic, but many streets are closed to cars, and the boardwalk is nice. The town itself is not "beautiful" in the way most of Italy is beautiful. The people, however, were some of the most beautiful and kind I have ever met. Marianna, my co-worker, brought me with her to meet her family. They were Lovely and I felt fortunate to be in this place and to experience the "real Italian" life that is unknown to so many tourists.

We went to the beach the first morning we were there. I went running, Marianna walked, and we met up at the end. I placed my hands in the Adriatic Sea, which was saltier than I expected, and marveled at the fact that I was facing Yugoslavia. The sand here was truly sandy, it felt good, even on my wimpy feet. The water lapped at my feet while they sank into the sand, and I looked out at the rocks that formed barriers for the boats. How different this felt than the previous week, on the other side of the country! I liked it very much.

That day was Marianna's birthday. I felt lucky to be a part of the celebration. We explored the city on foot after the early morning beach running, and had lunch with her grandmother and her sister. It was a relaxing, nice day. The two of us grabbed some pizza for dinner, which we ate at the beach, and then we joined her friends for gelato, and then for a drink at the pub.

Inside Rome

I went for a run and happened upon the Italian Geographic Society. Attached to the Geographic Society is a park, which sits atop a large hill. On Saturday, I went out early in the day and as I reached the top of this path, going blindly and not knowing where it would lead, I found the most amazing overlook of the ruins in the center of the city, just as the sun burst through the sky. It was literally breathtaking. I stopped moving, leaned against the stone wall, and watched as the amazing colors of pink, orange, yellow and a brilliant purple shone over the sky and highlighted, just for me it seemed, the beauty that is and was Rome. I have been fortunate to have had a few of those breathtaking-type moments—seeing the North Rim of the Grand Canyon at daybreak, for example—and this moment could have compared with any of them. What a wonderful thing to be breathless, not from being out of shape or from breathing bad air, but from beauty.

6

Medical Problems in a Foreign Country

You can't say I didn't see most of Rome. I took it upon myself to see parts of Rome that few tourists witness, not that they would want to. While I was in Italy, well, I had some problems. Most of these problems had to do with going to the bathroom. You may be tempted to skip this section, and I can't say that I would blame you. I include it here, though, because it really was a part of my experience abroad. It was not an aspect I would wish on anyone else, though I am thankful for it because it gave me perspective, and a pretty good story, I think.

Italian Hospitals

I had a little adventure this weekend, one I wasn't planning. I would not have voluntarily chosen this, but since it happened, I will share with you what I learned....

I spent a night in a hospital in Rome. Not a huge deal in the whole scope of all things medical, just some internal bleeding for some unknown reason. So—a whole night to drink a ton of icky stuff, and I do mean a ton—4 liters of the stuff, what made me gag from the first sip. The nurses were on me to "Beve!" (Drink!). That was followed by a full night of trips to the restroom to "clean me out." Luckily for you, I will spare you the details, but trust me when I tell you this was not nice. This was followed by much "exploring" the next day, with several different tests.

I had 8 nuns wait on my while I was in the hospital, for about 24 hrs. They wanted to chat with me, and since half of them were Polish and noted my last name on the register, they presented themselves and spoke to me in Polish. When I indicated, in Italian, that I didn't speak Polish, they would each make comments similar to "I can't believe you don't speak Polish with a name like that."

Interesting, in the U.S. it is never assumed that I would actually speak the language of my surname—but here that is very much the case.

I would never have imagined there were so many ways to dress like a nun. Here in Rome, I have probably witnessed 15 different sets of attire worn by these women. Their role in the hospital was unclear to me. I am sure they sat and prayed with the sick, but they also made beds, took blood pressure and temperatures, and generally seemed to be in charge. I asked the nun who was taking my blood pressure if she was also a nurse. She seemed aghast at that, which made me think, "OK, probably not…"

The hospital was a like a hotel. No white walls and sterile looking surfaces—this had dark wood molding and nice, colorful appliances. I truly thought I had entered the wrong place, not a hospital. No doctors wore white uniforms, or green or blue scrubs like you see in the States. They dressed very nicely, in expensive threads that it seems all Italians wear. For any of you ER fans, the doc that is from Europe—that guy was my doctor. I swear, just like him.

Luckily, I had an interpreter. My advisor came with me because the thought of going to the doctor and having to discuss my health issues, especially these health issues, was overwhelming. I hadn't yet learned the vocabulary to tell the doctor what exactly was happening inside my body. I was glad she was there, repeatedly.

An interesting concept—in Italy, they have social medicine and it is free. I checked into that and would have had to wait a month to get in. That didn't seem like a good idea given the situation. But heck, if you need to actually go into a hospital, how many situations can really wait a month? This hospital expects payment upon entry—no credit cards accepted, only cash or checks. I can see why this "private hospital" was able to give me such great care…

Medical issues

I got some frustrating news today about my health. My doctor wants me to have more tests done, the results that I have that I have been awaiting for 2 weeks have finally arrived and they are inconclusive. I continue to bleed internally, the doctors don't know exactly why, what is causing it, or how to fix it. I have a solitary rectal ulcer, they are sure, but they don't know what else, so I need to be "probed" again. I have been told to drink a lot of water and to make sure I am eating protein to fight the anemia I am facing from losing blood. The pain and discomfort that I experience when going to the bathroom has continued and the medications don't seem to be doing much in the way of treatment or helping the symptoms.

The fact that I received this news from my advisor and not from the doctor directly is another source of annoyance for me. I absolutely know that her heart is in the right place, and that it is difficult to play multiple roles—interpreter, advisor, and now "mother"—a role that she says comes naturally to her and that she would want someone to fill if her daughter were in the same situation (incidentally, her daughter is attending school in the U.S., far away from home as well). I appreciate all she has done for me, yet I was left feeling frustrated. They are many questions that popped into my mind that I immediately wanted to ask my doctor. The fact that I couldn't, and that he was not available to me, was disheartening, disturbing, and annoying. I am an educated health care consumer. I have done this doctor routine more than a few times. The fact that I am treated like a child and not told the condition of my own health is beyond my comprehension. I don't know why it has been like this—I can only speculate that it is a combination of the Italian system, of not being a native speaker of the language, of having someone who did speak Italian attend my appointments with me—which made me seem like a child in the eyes of the doctor.

My doctor left today to go on vacation. He will return on March 3rd, and I am supposed to be prepared to go to the hospital that day. I have already waited 2 weeks for results, and now I am supposed to wait 2 more, and then more testing, and then—dare I assume, another 2 weeks for results? What should I do in the meantime?

If you have been in my life for any length of time, you know that I have a few different medical issues. I wanted to leave this behind me. I wanted my time in Italy, 5 short months, to be free from hospitals, tests, and health problems. Dealing with this here, in this different system, with different rules and expectations, not to mention a different language, is more difficult. I don't want it to be difficult. I want it over.

I call a do-over. I would like to trade this body in for another. No, I am not asking for an "upgrade." I am not asking for smaller hips or a clearer complexion. Just a body that works right would be fine, thanks. I don't think the warrantee should be up with this one yet. Some parts seem to be wearing out sooner than they should, you see. They have laws against cars that are "lemons" in some states, seems the same should be available for bodies. Once you reach a certain level of damage and repairs, it is cheaper to turn it in and get a new one. I don't know how much a new body costs, but I am guessing that, given my medical expenses and the amount that insurance will not pay, it really would be less expensive for me to just get a new body than to go on living in this one. I am under 30, and I don't qualify for independent insurance—been turned down by 3 different companies because I am a "high-risk". This is not like the car whose engine burns up because somebody forgot to out oil in it. No—the maintenance stuff is there—I run and hike and stay active. I generally eat well though I do appreciate the occasional sweet, and I have cut out dairy because it is bad for my rheumatoid arthritis, and don't eat much meat—save for the visits home to my family. I don't smoke and never have. I drink in moderation, and what I have been drinking here has been red wine—isn't that supposed to be good for you? I take actions to deal with stress and strive to have balance in my life. Nope—this body is not falling apart out of neglect. It just doesn't seem to work quite right. So I am ready to trade this one in—when do you think the new one will be ready?

I have found some differences in the American and Italian cultures in terms of dealing with medical issues. There seems to be no need or desire for confidentiality here. In American, if this same situation were occurring, I envision concerned friends asking, "So how are *things?*" They would show concern, but would not likely ask direct questions about such sensitive and personal problems. The same has not been true thus far in Italy. I am asked regularly by well meaning and caring co-workers if there is still blood in my stool, where it hurts when I go to the bathroom, even what it feels like. Just two days ago, at a conference among psychology professionals, one person asked if I was feeling better. When I said, "A little bit," the others in the conversation, including many people that I had not met prior to this conference, asked what had been making me not feel good. This co-worker did not hesitate in responding that I had blood in my stool and had been in the hospital. My thoughts—"Hi. Nice to meet you, my name is Amy…now you know my story." I think this directness has impacted me—I am not feeling very shy about my health issues right now, as you might have gathered from the sharing of this story.

There is one redeeming thing here, if you get my sense of humor. You want to know the typical way to heal a rectal ulcer…to use a Gore–Tex patch. Isn't that funny? Well, I thought so. I imagined all that stuff inside me just "slipping on by" the patch. Cracked me up. Gore-Tex makes my boots waterproof, it just might do something for my insides.

Since this is supposed to be a "learning experience" I will share with you some of what I have learned as a result of bleeding from my butt:

1. *Ano*—the Italian word for anus. Not to be confused with *anno*, the word for year. The doc asked a question about my *ano*, and I indicated that no, I would only be here for 5 months, not a whole year.

2. *Fare feci*—literally, to make poop. Here, relieving yourself isn't passive—you actually "do it"—sort of a sense of pride, wouldn't you say? It should be something to be proud of—this "going to the bathroom thing" isn't all that easy, at least not for me right now.

3. *Troppo giovane per emorroidaria*—too young for hemorrhoids. Yes. Thank you. I heard this phrase repeatedly while I was having the colonoscopy. It was if they were saying, "hemorrhoids would be the easy answer, but she is too young, so there must be something else." Indeed. I agree.

Scoping

First, I have to give you the setting. It is the Italian hospital where I have now been several times. These same doctors had seen me before. They are speaking in Italian about other people's bowels. Luckily, my Italian is not so good that I can understand it without concentrating, so I tuned them out completely, but only after I learned that Senior Castellini, or was it Castalino, or maybe it was Castolina—whatever, he had to have a colonoscopy and it had gone bad—they punctured a hold right through him. I just didn't want to hear that before I got scoped. So—I stopped listening.

Instead of listening, I started watching. I was watching the group of four men preparing for this procedure. I watched as they cleaned equipment, arranged materials, and began preparing to invade my body once again. The next thing I know, the video screen comes on. This screen is hooked up to the probing camera that will be used to check out my innards. I see on the screen what looked like fibers, and look back to see that one of the doctors is cleaning the camera and the fibers that I see are a very close-up picture of the towel. OK. I am still not listening because now they are talking about how Seniorina somebody (I didn't catch the name, but I would place odds 100 to 1 that it ended in an "a," "e," "i," or "o"). I think it is fascinating to watch this camera, as though were my own eye looking around at things I couldn't see from my "prone and ready position" on the table. I witnessed one doctor pick his nose while the others weren't looking (I watched to make sure he wasn't touching me anywhere private!), and I saw another older, very distinguished-looking doctor pull his underwear out and readjust himself while the others were facing me. He was, in fact, distinguished—head of the department. What do you know? I am watching all of this, and containing my laughter, but barely.

Then the picture on the screen changes, and it is me. It is my whole backside—right there, on the screen. I was thinking, "I have never seen this part of myself." Sure you can stand in the mirror and look over your shoulder and get an idea, or you can use the department store mirrors at different angles to see how something fits, but all of a sudden I was looking at myself—directly from the back, and I was naked and lying on a table.

Now, usually I think I am pretty "grown up" about these things. But really, this was too much. I could see the doctor behind walking closer and closer to me. The *Jaws* theme came to my mind—you know, "Dadum, dadum, dadum…" It looked like an attack. I started laughing—except that I was trying not to laugh, which made my eyes water. The doctors, though I didn't know it at the time, were talking about what other "procedures" they planned to do to me. These Italian, distinguished-looking, old men thought I was crying. They all came over and tried to comfort me. Only one spoke English, the others knew a few words, so they were asking the "English-speaking" doctor to help them. This was funny to me. "Come sei dice, che OK?" (How do you say, "It is OK?")—OK is the same in both languages—this was hilarious. Not to mention that now all 4 doctors were standing by my face and the camera had been place on the table—directly facing my anus. While they are discussing how to stop me from crying, all I see is a very large, close-up picture of my rear end. The "English-speaking" doctor didn't speak that great of English, because he responded to the other doctors that he did not know how to say OK in English. I am laughing so hard; I almost fall off of the table. They don't really notice at first, because they are debating linguistics, but then one notices, taps the others on the shoulders and they all look at me. I have tears running down my face, I couldn't stop laughing at that moment if you paid me. They decide that words wouldn't do, so they all come closer and patted my head. One of them pinched my cheeks. You know how much I like this…and I think it is interesting that a doctor would do such a thing. "First these cheeks, then the others," I say to myself—can you see why this was funny to me?

The doctors are debating if they should go ahead with this procedure—after all, I seem more upset than they have ever seen before. I am thinking about the "cleaning out" I have had to do the night before and again that morning, and no way am I leaving without them doing this procedure. I tried to explain that I was laughing, not crying, and one of them says, "But you have water in the eye, not giggle in the belly." Don't go there, dude, my belly giggling is an off-limits topic for you, thank you! Then I think of my dad, who has a great laugh—he hardly makes any noise at all, but his belly goes up and down. Us "kids" all love it, and laugh whenever he does, whether what he said was funny or not (Sorry, Dad, but sometimes your jokes just really aren't all that funny…but we love you anyway). So then I try to sing the *Jaws* tune for the docs, to help explain why I was laughing…but I guess that movie didn't come to Italy—no recognition, only strange looks. Calm down—I tell myself. And then I got to see my insides….

Good news—I am healing. My ulcer seemed to be gone. It responded better to the medications than they had anticipated. There is only a small scar there now and I feel good. That night, I got to stop the medication. I slept a full 8 hours without waking—it had been 6 weeks since I had slept through a night without waking at least 3 times from the medication. It is hard to describe how good it felt to really sleep. I have to keep an eye on the problem. They aren't sure what caused it, though they said was likely linked to my immune system problems. My friends here blame the Italian food. Whatever—it is gone for now, and I am happy.

More problems with pooping

I guess every "story" needs its bad thing to happen—it makes the story more interesting. What readers would enjoy reading it if only good things occurred, right? The problem, of course, is that this story is my life. My health difficulties continue….

I have been asked to describe the "issues" that my colon is having. Think of pooping shards of glass, that is all I can say. Each time, it feels like new wounds are being opened in my insides. I can feel my face turning white and I feel faint. The feeling passes, but only after about an hour after each bowel movement. Makes me very glad I don't have diarrhea.

I am going to a different doctor, an English-speaking one. This situation is better, though the doctor has recommended the same treatment that I have already had, which worked—for about a week. I am left feeling like we are treating symptoms and not the cause. They don't know what is causing these problems and they aren't sure how to deal with them. I have been told, again, that I am "much too young" to have these kinds of problems. Looks like I will be having another scooping in the near future. I doubt it can be as fun as the last one, but I will keep you informed.

Money, Health Insurance, and Medical Bills up the Wazoo

In the U.S., we tend to not talk about money. It is rude to ask someone what their salary is, how much something cost them, or the level of their financial status. Not so in Italy—it is talked about frequently. I am going with the Italian custom right now...

Today I found out that my request for a loan to pay my medical expenses was denied from the Fulbright Commission. They suggested that I return to the U.S. for treatment because they don't want to pay for it. I have borrowed money from my advisor to pay my medical bills, because the hospital I went to did not accept my insurance (or credit cards—you had to pay in cash, ugh). She needs it back, and I don't have those kinds of funds. I have sold my blood in the past, but they don't pay for blood here in Italy. I am looking for other ways to make a quick buck...and selling drugs or prostituting is out of the question, given my history with the carabinieri, I would surely get caught. Kidding.

I am stuck this evening, pondering the Insurance/Medical Care/Socialized Medicine issue. I don't know the best answer. I have heard amazing things about socialized medicine, and I have heard that it can be detrimental. I do know this—the current system is not good and needs to be changed. I am a graduate student, living off of loans and my meager earnings—despite working four jobs over the last year. How am I supposed to have $4000 in cash to pay for medical expenses? Yes, it is true that the Fulbright Commission provides me with insurance. The problem here is that same that I have encountered in the States—you are supposed to get reimbursed—which assumes you have that money before you go to the doctor. If I had that kind of money lying around, I might not need the insurance....

Maybe I shouldn't write when I feel so frustrated with this. Or maybe that is when I most need to write—to get this out and vent my frustrations at a system that does not work for those who most need it. I am not someone who is trying to "live off the system." I am working hard to gain the education that I need to be a productive part of society. I am not asking for a handout, just for some understanding and support when I most need it. Insurance that actually pays for one's medical expenses would be a good start.

I have been told many times "money doesn't matter, what matters is your health." Well, my health sucks. I am trying to get that taken care of, but the money issues are preventing me from getting what I need, and causing me a lot of distress in the meanwhile. I am in no way talking about wanting to be rich here, just wanting insurance that actually paid for medical services. I am making decisions about my health based on finances. "Should I have that procedure—no wait, I can't afford it." "Maybe I should see a specialist in the US, no wait—I won't have insurance there until July when I start internship...guess it will have to wait until then..." "I think I need to go to the doctor, but I don't have the money to pay for it. I can only withdraw $200 from my credit card a day. If I make an appointment for next week, let's see, I can take out $200 a day for 8 days...I wonder if that will be enough?" This is wrong. Ugh, ugh, ugh.

Update: My colon is doing somewhat better now. Thanks for asking.

7

On the Importance of Friends

I learned a few things about friends while I was away. The first is that true friends are always there for you. We all have heard that, but know it. Trust it. Don't be afraid to ask for help when you need it. You just might find that your friends really want to help and don't feel burdened with your "stuff." The second is that friendships can be built in many ways, and that each and every friend is important in his or her own way. Cherish them all and be thankful for who they are, what they give to you, and the lessons that you learn through them.

Friends

After about 2 months of being in Rome and doing a great deal of exploring on my own, a comment was made that went straight to my heart. Someone that I love and that loves me commented that, although it sounded as if I was having a lot of fun, I was doing most of it all alone. Didn't that bother me? Did I ever wish I had friends in Italy to share it with?

Until the moment that was said, I could honestly say, "No." It hadn't bothered me in the least, because I had been meeting new people everyday and having interesting conversations. I also enjoy the solo travel. But when that was said to me, I realized that I didn't have anyone here with whom I could share my medical news, no one to listen to me vent my frustration, and no one with whom I felt comfortable enough to share my tears. I have met some great people here who are becoming friends, people that I have lunch with and make plans with in the evenings, but no one that I have opened up to in that way. After that phone conversation, I felt lonely for the first time since I arrived. Being alone is fine, I like it and sometimes prefer it, though I cherish and appreciate the friends that I have. Being lonely is another matter. A sad one.

I realize that building friendships is not necessarily related to time spent together, a lesson I learned well from my dear friend Sarah, from England, with whom I spent one intense month in Siena. In that time we shared a lot. It was that sharing that brought us together, in addition to the time spent, which created a friendship. Sarah and I would have not become that close had I not opened up to her in order to share things with her. I think it is up to me to do the same here, to open up and take my acquaintances to a deeper level. Why haven't I shared this with Cristina, the wonderful woman I work with from Brazil, who has lunch with me frequently and whom I really enjoy? I think part of it is of course the uncomfortable feelings that arise when talking about these types of health issues. The other part has been not wanting to talk about them—not wanting to deal with them, and intentionally trying to "keep it light." At the same time, though, I long for that intimacy, to share what I am going through with someone who is here, some one who can hold my hand and tell me it will be OK.

Progress report: I almost deleted what I wrote above. Reading it now, it sounds awful. I am OK, really—just exploring what I was feeling at the time. After that entry, I called a person here that I have hung out with a couple of times, and we had dinner. It was a great dinner, and I shared with her what is happening with my health. She shared with me some of her current challenges as well, and thanked me for calling. It seems she was looking for someone to talk to that day as well. It felt like we were no longer just acquaintances, rather we were becoming *friends*.

After dinner, we met up with some other people that she knows, and helped an Italian celebrate his birthday. We went to an amazing dance club—on a houseboat on the river. The club is exclusive; you have to have your name on the guest list to be allowed on the boat. Since we were with Birthday Boy, it was no problem. We stayed out very late, dancing until dawn. The nearly full moon shining over the Tiber river was quite a sight. The Italian men mostly wore their shirts unbuttoned about half-way down their chests, while the women's skirts were more than half-way up their thighs. The come-on line that was used on me more than once was "What's you sign?" I laughed out loud. Was this for real? It was. I thoroughly enjoyed myself. I have also talked with Cristina, the woman I mentioned above, and told her my situation over our shared picnic lunch in the park. She was wonderful and supportive, and I questioned why I hadn't shared this with her before. Cristina said that she would do anything she could to help me out with this. Then, she reached over and grabbed my hand, and told me that it would be all right. A new "*friendship*" was formed.

Spending International Women's Day with a Friend

Emily was here to visit! I had a vision of taking her around town and showing her the sights, without realizing that she had been to Rome and knew the sites already. It was fun to show her new monuments, new streets, and then she would say, "Oh yeah, we are near___, I remember this from before." It was a pseudo-tour, and it was great.

We found ourselves near the City Hall, which served as a backdrop for an exhibition for a work of art designed for Women's Day—"La giornata di le donne." This was widely celebrated throughout the city in commemoration of women's struggles for employment and safety standards. It began with the first Women's garment makers' movement in the U.S. I wondered what the celebrations were like in the States?

Emily and I walked through popular and "unknown" parts of Rome, talking and laughing and enjoying the day. Mid-afternoon found us at an outdoor café, refueling ourselves with some liquids in the artistic area of Trastevere. We laughed, caught up, shared stories, compared lives, and pondered many things. Emily has been living in Paris, and will soon go to Germany to stay for a while. We have a lot in common, in many ways, and I truly enjoyed the day we spent together. We ended our day with dinner out—which consisted of seafood pasta with shrimp, wonderful grilled sea bass, and ended with a mixed salad. (By the way, I get this desire to describe meals from my grandmother on my mother's side. Not only does she tell of her travels on the drives she has taken, but also she never forgets to include the important information, like where to buy the best caramel rolls, or which coffee shop has the best blackberry pie. What can I say—I am her offspring.)

With the architect and the art historian

I saw Rome this weekend in a way I never had before—through the eyes of two people—Jules and Emily—who really do "see" the world differently than I. It was neat to go with Jules to the area of Rome. It was his old "haunt" when he lived in Rome for a year to study architecture. I learned more about columns, facades, and famous Roman architects than I ever thought I would know—and all in two days with a great guide. From Emily, I have learned more art history than I thought I could remember about Rome and the artists that lived here, but seeing it with them, through them, and because of them, I was able to enjoy this place in a new way. Reading the facts that the two of them shared in a book would probably not have gotten my attention. This was living, teaching, learning and sharing.

One thing I learned from this experience is that there really are many different worlds, not simply "the world." There really is a world of art history, with its interesting tales and fascinating characters and beautiful works. There is also a world of architecture, with its myriad of buildings, stories, builders, and environment-shapers. The world of psychology is but one of many. I am so glad that "the world" encompasses these other worlds. I have learned a lot about many things that interest me. I am a questioner, a forever student. The more I learn, though, the more I realize there is so much more to be learned. At the end of the weekend, I felt as though I saw Rome in yet another light, and was thankful to my "teachers" for sharing their knowledge with me.

We had a great time. The three of us had lunch at Jules' old favorite place. The salads were great—large and wholesome. Then, the owner of the restaurant recognized Jules from his visits to this place 10 years ago, so we got free desserts—two each! One was chocolate and cake-like and yummy. The other was similar to a lemon tort, and was delicious as well (you have already been warned about my "food descriptions"!). Lunch was followed by an afternoon passagiata—walking all over—just looking at things and experiencing life. It was a gorgeous, sunny day, albeit quite breezy and chilly. Our wandering found us at the Tiber River, looking at the "Bridge of Statues" by Bernini. We followed the bridge across and arrived at the Castle San'Angelo (Castle of the Angles) and decided to go in.

I had wanted to see the inside of this castle, and had actually gone to it with that intent before, only to find that it was closed on Mondays (Hint to all travels to Rome—find out what day the sites are closed *before* you go). Jules thought he had been there before, but he didn't remember much about it. This castle has quite a history—dating from the 6th century. That is old. At one time it was a prison, housing the biggest hoodlums in Rome. It was later converted to a home for the Popes. I think that is great! It is said that Pope Gregory the Great saw a vision of an angel over the building, signaling the end of the plague, at which time it was given its current name. The castle was fascinating, with many rooms housing frescos and interesting paintings and works by famous people (I learned that from my guests!). I had envisioned a prison, and what I saw astounded me. It was gorgeous and old and intriguing. We arrived at the top of the castle in time to watch the sunset over the entire city. The wind was blowing and the clouds were rapidly changing their colors and form—from white to yellow to orange and then pink—and from puffy, billowy pillows to pulled cotton stretching across the horizon. It would have been difficult to convince me at that moment that I wasn't in the presence of angels, since I have heard they reside in heaven.

A friend from home

Caroline was here to visit! It was great to see her, to catch up, to just hang out, to go to new places with her, and to be in the company of a good friend. She is a super person, and I felt lucky to have the time to share this experience with her.

Caroline and I met when I arrived at Gallaudet, but she was in the class above me, so it took a little while for us to really get to know each other. After that first year, though, we have been out to listen to music many times, gone to a Bluegrass festival together and camped, spent many hours talking about life and sharing stories, and hung out with other people who share our common interests. I would stay with her on the evenings we went out for a late night on the town, and we would talk until morning. We have supported each other through the difficult aspects of our program, such as passing sign language evaluation test, and comprehensive exams. Caroline would often ride with me when we met other people or drove out to Annapolis, and we always had good discussions along the way. I have always known she was someone I could count on to share my woes with—and she came through for me each and every time.

Given all that, it was amazing to me how much more I felt that I had gotten to know Caroline during the week that she spent with me. It is nice to be able to spend time with a friend out of context. Even though I completely appreciated the mutual support we gave each other about school, it was nice to not have to talk about that now. I learned a lot about her, and have a greater appreciation for who she is, now that I know her on a different level. I am lucky to have a good friend that does not pass judgments, is very supportive, shows that she cares, and is fun to be around. Here's to you, Caroline—salute!

8

Abroad at a Time of War

The time I spent in Italy was the time that the U.S. was waging a war on Iraq. I am not generally in favor of war, though I admit to not knowing much about world politics and not getting heavily involved with these issues in the past. However, being in Italy during this time changed my views, forced me to look at the actions of my country, and awakened my desire to "do something" and fight for what I believed. I realize that many Americans were in support of that war effort. Many were not. In writing about this topic, I ask that you try to understand the influence of being in another land and seeing these world events through a different lens. Disagree with me if you will, but first, hear me.

Anti-Americanismo

St. Francis urged Assisi to serve as a "place of peace," and it has done so since his time, in the 13th century. Many talks occurred in this town during various civil unrests, including during World War II.

I arrived in Assisi on the day the entire world held marches for peace. On that day, Saddam Hussein's "#2 man"—Aziz, was visiting the Cathedral of St. Francis, following his visit with the Pope the day before. There were peace activists present for the rally. A large percentage of the windows in the narrow streets of Assisi flew rainbow-colored flags that said, "Pace"—which means peace.

I had planned to participate in this demonstration and show that I, as an American, am in support of peace. I don't know what actions should be taken to cure the world's problems, but I don't think that pre-emptive war is the answer. I am opposed to the manner in which the Bush administration has bullied other countries. I resent the fact that America is attempting to act alone in a problem that the world faces.

My arrival at the demonstration was not welcome by a few people, who immediately spotted me, knew that I was an American, and challenged me to defend the stance my country has taken. I was labeled "an American fascist" by one young man, and an "arrogant American who holds all the power" by another. I had not expected to necessarily be welcomed with open arms, but I certainly did not expect this either. I was at a loss for words, and felt afraid. I wanted to shout, "But I am here because I want peace"—but my Italian escaped me at that moment, and I said nothing. I did not want to speak in English, which I feared would only exacerbate this situation, because Europeans generally do not like that fact that Americans expect everyone to speak English, when many Americans have never attempted to learn another language. This is a big issue for them, and I knew it. I never felt in danger of my life, or truly at risk of physical retribution, but I was afraid nonetheless.

Luckily, another Italian man intervened and pointed out that the labeling that these young people (in their teen years) were doing was destructive to the purpose of the peace march. He was an eloquent speaker, and his Italian seemed to be "working" whereas mine had not yet recovered. He talked of the need for all people that were opposed to the war to stand up and be accounted for, and acknowledged that Americans against the war were of particular importance, in letting our government know where we stood. He quoted the newspaper and said that America is divided on the issue of the war aimed at Saddam Hussein, but that the majority of Americans are especially cautious of going to war without the backing of the UN. Then it was my turn to speak, and I explained to these young men my position, and my reasons for attending that march for peace.

That moment transformed me, them, and us. We talked about real issues—as individuals, not citizens of any particular country. They explained to me their frustration with the U.S. position of power, of its unwillingness to see itself as part a worldwide community, rather than the ruler of it. I explained the lack of information that Americans get from a media empire that does not show us the story of what is happening in the world, unless it directly impacts the U.S. Even then, I explained, the news we receive is sensationalized and is influenced by the financial backers of the media corporations. The Italians told me of their fears of an international war, the fear that Europeans have of not backing the United States, because it is "almighty" and has threatened those countries it no longer views as allies. I shared my concern that the world views the Bush administration as representing Americans, when in truth it represents no Americans that I know personally. I don't actually *know* people who are rich and have wealth handed down to them (are you aware that, in each job that George W. has held, he has *lost* money for the company for which he worked. He has never *made* money in his life), nor have I been part of the "good old boys club," nor do I understand the life of a person who lives on a ranch in Texas. It was a wonderful conversation. I felt my guard go down, which allowed them to see me for who I was. It also allowed me to truly take in what they were saying, and rather than feel defensive, as I had initially, I was able to better understand their perspectives. I thought to myself, "This it is what the Fulbright is supposed to be about—a cultural exchange that allows individuals to learn about another culture and share their knowledge of the culture from which they came, to better increase world understanding." That is what the literature said, and at this moment, it came true for me. My time here is not meant to solely conduct some research, it is much more vast than that. This does not only extend to my knowledge of Italy and its inhabitants, but to others who are also non-American. My eyes had been opened, yet again.

The book I am currently reading, "Why do people hate America?" shines further light on this issue. (I highly recommend this book for anyone brave enough to really challenge themselves, their thinking about nationalism, and what it means to be an American today.) When the top 3 richest Americans make more money than the poorest 48 countries, one can see why the world is frustrated. The U.S. refused to sign the Kyoto Protocol to help reduce global warming, even though Americans use more than 50% of the world's natural resources. In a period of just 2 years alone, the U.S. has been the sole opponent in over 150 proposals brought forth to the United Nations, claiming they would not serve to better our economic standing. These proposals had to do with furthering human rights, peace, economic justice, nuclear disarmament, and apartheid. *Every other member of the U.N. voted for these proposals, and the U.S. voted against them*, indicating they were not in ***our*** best interests.

My experience at the beginning of the peace march in Assisi left me to ponder what it must have been like to be an Arab American in the U.S. following the 9-11 attacks. I know that my experience does not compare to the hatred expressed toward and the actions taken against some of those individuals, but I did feel that it gave me just a *sense* of what it was like to be labeled as part of my "group." However, my sentiments do not coincide with that of my group at all on this issue, if you think that my group is the Bush administration. I am not trying to downplay the experiences of those people at all. I just felt like I came one step closer to understanding the racism and prejudice that is still alive in America, and I knew what it was like to be a citizen of a country that is not liked throughout the world.

My country is at war

I don't want to debate the merits of war at this time. I am living in a country where that debate happens constantly. I hope only to share my experiences living in another country at a time when the United States has started another war...I am the only American at my place of work. Since the U.S. began talk of pre-emptive war, I have been questioned about the stance of my country. Since the war became a reality, I have been in a position to answer for our actions. I don't know how to do that. For the most part, my co-workers are truly interested in understanding the American perspective, because they are truly puzzled as to why a country would want to go to war.

I recall being in a history class in college, a class that was made up of mostly Caucasian individuals, a few students of Asian decent, and one African-American. It was clear to me at that time that it was not fair to question this individual as to "why all Blacks...." How should he know? Certainly he had may have had access to insights that some of us would never know. Yet, how could that professor ask him to speak for "his people?" I was sure that the perspectives of African Americans differed and could not be answered by only one person. I had a discussion with that classmate about his experience as "the voice of his people" and how uncomfortable it was for him.

I have not been asked about the history of slavery, or what I think of Martin Luther King, Jr., but I have been asked to defend the United States in its constant involvement in conflict. Not a year has gone by in the last 25 years, when we have not bombed someplace. I don't have the answers. I was asked this week to explain the perspective of Americans on Kosovo. Hummm...There was a study conducted this last year that asked 100 Americans to explain the reasons we were involved with Kosovo, 90 of them could not answer. Of those that didn't know the answer to the above question, the number one answer given was "it was probably related to money." Hummm again.

Italians don't like Saddam. I realize I am making a sweeping generalization here, and that there are exceptions. However, the Italians that I have met think he is nuts. They don't want to see him in office, but they don't see him as a threat the way the U.S. seems to view him. They are also terrified of the U.S. having the power to say "screw off" to the rest of the world and do what it wants anyway. They believe that if this is allowed to continue happening, Italy could be next. I saw a sign the other day that said, "A fanatic that *might have weapons* is safer than a fanatic with *more weapons* than anyone else in the world." One Italian told me that, for him, standing up for Iraq is like standing up for the other little kids in class that are being picked on by the class bullies. You may not like the "geek" any more than the next guy, but compared to the bully, who has also bullied you in the past, he seems OK.

One co-worker pulled out a map yesterday. He is concerned that the U.S. will bomb Italy. Why you might ask? What do we have against Italy? Look at your own map. Bosnia, Slovenia and Croatia lie across the Adriatic from Italy. Think of the distance between New York and the North Caroline, or between Seattle, Washington and Eugene, Oregon—these countries are even closer. When war is close by, it seems more real. Not to mention that Italy borders Austria, Germany, and France—which have all seen war as well. The Middle East isn't so far away...

On the evening that the bombing began, I was walking home from doing an interview with a family. I hadn't expected what I saw—the carabinari (police) were everywhere. People were all over the streets. Protesters were carrying signs, marchers were chanting. There was an incredible amount of energy in the air. I was approached by two carabinari and asked if I was American. I told them that I was, and they took me home. They told me it was unsafe for me to walk by myself that evening. I had not been afraid because I was American. I felt safe. My experience with my European friends is that they are quite good at separating the people from the governments. It is the American government they are protesting, not the American people. In fact, I think they are better at making that distinction that many Americans are (remember the anti-Arab sentiments following 9-11?). I have been able to explain myself in these situations and I have felt that they really listened. On this night, however, I was escorted home. The police believed that the anger, the fear felt by many Italians that night, would not allow me to talk my why out of confrontations. I was not afraid. I did not think that anything would happen; the protesters were energized, but not violent. The police disagreed and insisted that I leave the scene.

When I arrived home, I felt sad. Americans had begun killing people. I am American. Against my will, and my protests, my government had begun taking action. It is easy to think of the conflicts we have been involved with as "somewhere over there." Yet all Americans felt the impact when the Twin Towers, the Pentagon, and some farmland in Pennsylvania were hit by planes. I know that some people think this is reason in and of itself to "get back." Yet I question—how could we ever do that to other people? What of the people that lived in, worked in, and thought of Baghdad as their home? I was very, very sad indeed.

9

Thoughts on Italian Culture

Italy has a culture all its own. Northern Italy is different from Southern Italy, all Italians will tell you. Yet, there are some interesting similarities. I have noted a few incidents that are "unique" and would not be likely to occur in the U.S. There were so many aspects of the culture, though, and some of those cultural intricacies became my own. At the least, they became harder to see as I was "acculturated" to the Italian system. Here are just a few that stand out in my mind:

Thoughts on change

Italians and Americans differ on their thoughts on change. I mean their thoughts on coins, and using them to pay for things. I don't think Americans want to deal with it. Several times in the U.S., I have been making a purchase, and said, "Just a second, I think I have the change," to which the cashier has said, "That it is OK, I don't need it." The cashier then punches in the amount you handed over, and the automatic coin counter dispenses your money. Change in Italy has a different quality altogether.

I was at the market the other evening here in Rome. The person at the start of the line did not have the appropriate change, so the cashier asked the next person in line if she had the correct change to help this poor man, whom I believe was German, and did not seem to understand this whole thing about the change. He tried indicating to the cashier that he had enough money, that his bill had come to 11,43 Euro and he had given her 15,00 Euro. I believe that he was offended that she was asking others to help him out, as he pointed out again, in broken Italian, that he had enough money and did not need the charity. After this difficult transaction ended, I breathed a sigh of relief, "OK, we are moving on to the next one." Normally, there are no more than 2 or 3 people in line at a time at the little market where I shop. This evening it was different, and I was the 6th in line, behind people who were making large purchases.

The next person in line was a short woman who was considerably older. I noted her shortness because I looked down on her and noticed that she had a bald spot on the top of her head, and I noticed her oldness because—well, she was old and looked it. She was cute, smiley, and had very kind eyes. I guessed that she makes frequent stops at the market and buys only a little, just what she can carry to her home in her shopping bag. This lady's total came to 8.32 Euro. She did not have the right change. The cashier asked the next person in line, who contributed 10 cents, then the next, who also gave 10 cents. Two more people were able to contribute 5 cents each. One of them had a 20 cent piece, but that would have pushed the total past 32 cents, and the cashier was not interested in going above the specified amount, even if she could have given some change from that in her hand. It was up to me, 5 people back, to come up with the 2 cents. I gave it to the cashier, and the older lady smiled broadly at me. I was happy to be of help, to finally allow her to take her groceries and leave.

The thing was, there were still 4 people ahead of me, and I knew what awaited. The cashier wanted to "credit" each person with their contribution, "You gave 10 cents, so I will take that off your total at the end." Wouldn't you know it, but the time I had contributed my change to the people ahead of me, I was 2 cents short of the required change when it came to be my turn to pay for my purchases. I found this funny. I was the only one that did, though, since this is a normal and typical interaction for the people that live here. The benefit was that those of us in line acted as community, working together. We celebrated when we finally gathered enough money for each person's purchase. I don't think that was the intended purpose of the somewhat grumpy cashier that evening, but that is what I took away from it, anyway—that and the advice to "bring lots of change."

Small Towns on Sundays

My suggestion is—don't go. I love small towns, I enjoy exploring, and I have the notion that I will meet more friendly people in a small place. The problem, though, is that on Sundays, in Italy, nothing is open. No one is out, and small towns are not easily accessible.

I share this with you from experience. A couple of weeks ago, I went to Viterbo, a small town in the Lazio region—in which Rome resides. It wasn't far away. My thought was that since I was only doing a day trip and not a weekend trip, it would be good to go to a nearby small town. That trip included a long walk to the metro stop outside of town (because the buses don't run on Sundays), a train ride, followed by another bus ride, and I had to wait 55 minutes for the next bus, because they don't run very regularly on Sundays. Upon reaching the bus terminal near Viterbo, I was required to take a taxi to actually get to the town. This town, "close by and easy to visit" took longer to get to than a trip to Florence or Bologna would have!

You would think I would have learned my lesson with that, right? But it was a couple of Sundays ago, and I must have attributed the delays to being an unfortunate circumstance. Nope. Today I went to Anagni. Again, I only had Sunday available, so I didn't want to plan a long trip that would require a whole weekend. My guidebook said that this town was "directly on the train line leaving from Termini." The station itself was on the direct train line, and it did have the same name as the town I was trying to get to, but when I arrived, I saw that the sign said "Anagni—8 kilometers." Hmmm. I read the bus schedule posted on the wall—no bus service on Sundays. No taxis in the town—too small. I pondered my options, and decided to walk to town (roughly 4.5 miles). After a treacherous walk—mainly due to the speedy traffic, lack of pedestrian walkway, and cars that were no used to people walking on this country road—I arrived at the edge of town. I asked one young man how far it was to the "centro." From behind the van he was standing near, 10 other young men came out to look at this crazy person who was even asking such a thing. I had an entire calcio team (soccer) laughing at the fact that I would have even considered visiting this small town, let alone the fact that I had already walked from the train station to there. They thought I was crazy, literally. Yep, Anagni has a medieval town center, but that would be another 8 km in. And then the walk back...I didn't go on. I would have likely missed the train back to Rome, and did not want to stay the night in this town, didn't even think it would have places for me to stay, in fact. Seems I have learned a lesson—what *not to do* with my Sundays in Italy.

My dining experience

Speaking of food—Emelio Reggio is called the "gastronomic capital of the world"—and is the pride of Italian cooking. Here is where parmesan cheese is made, and the best wines in Italy (depending on who you ask!) come from here or Tuscany. In the area of Rome, food is prepared with olive oil. In Emelio-Reggio they make it with butter. With one exception, when I order a plate of spinach here, I have not tasted butter since I arrived. I was almost not prepared for that again! Did you know that *tortellini* is actually pasta stuffed with meat, whereas *tortalloni* is pasta stuffed with cheese? I had never known there was a difference.

I had an amazing dinner at a great restaurant that was also a piano bar. I arrived late in the afternoon, and did a lot of wandering around, checking things out and finding a hotel. By 8:45 p.m., I was hungry and ready for dinner. I was the first person in the restaurant—and they asked why I came to eat so early. I am familiar with the Italian dinnertime, but usually by 8pm there is someone else in the room! I had waited until almost 9pm just in case, at which point the strawberries I had for lunch where no longer providing me any nourishment. So—the waiter, very cute, very Italian, very friendly—felt sorry for me because I was the only person, and he gave me his undivided attention. When the first plate came out, he sent it back and demanded more. Not what I needed, but who could argue with that? The second plate arrived, and he indicated that the chef would need to feed me more if he wanted a happy customer. "Basta" I insisted, this was enough. Others began to arrive, and the musician began playing sappy love songs in Italian. Translated, they don't mean as much, but in Italian they sound so wonderful, so melodic, so flowing. One song, once I listened closely, said, "I love you more than I love spaghetti." OK—so I didn't listen so closely after that. But a young lady eating alone is a spectacle in Italy, deserving of much attention. The musician played song after song and dedicated them to me. Oh my. The scattered couples looked at me, and then went back to kissing over their pasta, and one group of women looked at me glaringly. One woman walked by, put her hand on my shoulder, and asked, "How did you get that cute waiter to be so nice to you?" Nice? He is making me eat all this stuff! No, really, he was very nice. After the mandatory dessert, he brought me limoncello. I like that stuff. I learned about it on my first visit to Italy, when I visited the Amalfi coast. It is good. Noting that I liked it, the waiter refilled my glass a few times, never saying a word, just smiling and nodding encouragement. I informed the singer that I needed to be going, and thanked him for his music. He said, "One more, seniorina." This song really was nice, not corny like some of the others, and it was very romantic. That was my send-off for the night. I left feeling full from dinner, tingly from the liquor, content from having this experience in this new place, and melancholy from the absence of my loved ones. I walked to my hotel under a blanket of stars and wondered if he was out there too, looking at the moon.

A foiled plan

Ok, so I was on a train…all stories of foiled trips in Italy begin this way, I think. In keeping with traditions, I will begin…So I was on this train, headed to Bologna, where I needed to change trains to get to my true destination, Reggio Emelia. I had taken the 5:45am train out of Rome, with plans to arrive at my final destination at 10:15am, giving me enough time to find where I needed to go and arrive by my 11am scheduled meeting. Up until Bologna, everything had gone as planned. My train arrived a bit early, and I needed to use the restroom, so I headed to the bathroom, after checking in the main station to find which platform I would need to go to for the next train. Number 8. Ok, perfect. I finished taking care of business, and headed out to stand and wait for my train.

On the platform, I double-checked to be sure that the train I was getting on was headed in the right direction. Yep—everything was going as planned. I found a seat and commenced the reading of the materials I had brought along to prep for this meeting. As we approached 10am, the train guy (I don't know his title) came along to check boarding passes. He said, "That is the wrong ticket, please get out your other one." I looked at my ticket, which indicated that my final destination was Reggio Emelia. I said, "I think this is right, sir, Reggio Emelia is where I want to go." He said, "Well, then your ticket may be right, but the train you are on is wrong. You are going to Florence." Florence?!? I had already been to Florence that morning, at about 7:30am, on my way to Bologna. What? The lady sitting next to me said, "Yes, didn't you hear the announcement at the train station that they were changing platforms? The Reggio Emelia train was moved to platform 6." No I did not hear that! I was in the restroom, where they don't have a speaker, and what was audible was certainly not discernable. I didn't understand any of that. "But the platform said it was going the right way." "Yes, but they changed that information inside the stations to indicate that they changed platforms at the last minute." Oh…

Have you ever felt like a fool? I was in a cabin with 3 Italians, all shaking their heads. I felt like a big fool. The train guy at first said I would have to pay for the ticket to Florence from Bologna—which was more than the ticket from Bologna to Reggio Emelia. I looked at him with wide-eyes. I had a meeting at 11am. I was supposed to be in Reggio Emelia. What should I do now? He was kind and generous, and told me to just have a seat, and not to worry. He changed his mind about charging me for the extra "trip" I had taken, because he said he could clearly see that I was not trying to pull one over on him. Was it the sad look in my eyes, the confusion on my face, or the slump in my shoulders? I don't know.

He took pity on my, and just watched me as I sat back in my seat and wondered about my options. He returned a few minutes later with the schedule of all trains leaving from Florence. He wrote down for me the number of the next train that I needed to take, instructions on where I would need to switch trains, and information about how much time I would have between each. I appreciated his extra effort and forced a smile.

OK. I had a plan. I would call the woman I was supposed to meet with as soon as I arrived in Florence. I would tell you about my situation and let her know I would be there around 1:30pm. It would all be OK; we would still have the afternoon to meet. All I needed to do was make sure I caught the train leaving from Florence 5 minutes after we arrived. I was told which platform to go to, and the number, so I was sure I could do it. And then…our train stopped. It just didn't move any more. We were 15 minutes from Florence, and having "technical difficulties." Don't you hate that? OK—maybe I can still make it….

We sat for 15 minutes. The train I needed to take was gone. I was in Florence, hours away from my destination. I had been traveling since 5:45 a.m., and it was now 12:15pm. It only takes 1 ½ hrs to get to Florence by train, if you take a more direct route. UGH. The next train going to Reggio Emelia would not get me there until 5 p.m. I had to be back in Rome the next day. What should I do? I tried to call my contact in R-E, to no avail. I resigned myself to the fact that I would not see that part of Italy on that day. I found an internet café at the station, and sent a message indicating that the day had not gone quite (at all) as planned. On to Plan B…

The biggest meal of my life

Italians are infamous for their large dinners. I have had more than my fair share of them since I arrived. Several courses are served, first pasta, then a meat dish, followed by a side dish, vegetables, and cheese. Next come the fruit, the dessert, and the café. That is normal. What I experienced on this day was anything but….

I went away for the weekend, with Marianna and her family. The interesting part was that Marianna was already in the town where we were going, so I rode in a car with her parents—the entire width of the country, to meet up with her. "I have never met them before—so this was going to be interesting," I thought as I waited for them to arrive in their car that I was told was red—my only clue to finding them.

I met Marianna's parents at the train station, and rode with them through an amazing national park, where we saw a bear, and on to a tiny town on the eastern side of the Apennine mountains. Along the way, her father pointed out the town of his birth, a small city in the middle of the country that was never under Roman rule. The Romans could not take over this city, despite the immense spread of their Empire. He told me this story with pride, as though he himself had fought back Caesar Augustus. As my tour guide, he showed me the largest mountain in the Apennines chain, told me about the natural resources of the area, and explained the festivals and celebrations that take place in this area of Italy. We drove together, the three of us, through a gorgeous park, with snow-covered peaks all around. This area is not accessible by train, so I had never visited, despite its relative proximity to Rome. That was part of the beauty of it, I think, that there were no tourists. I was not going to some "destination," just simply traveling through this green, vast, tall, clear, bright range of mountains to visit some friends of their family. Marianna and her sister had been on vacation, and were to meet us in this tiny town high up in the mountains for "lunch."

Their friends were gracious and kind, welcoming and open. I liked them immediately. They wanted to show me their home, to show me their town, and to make me feel welcome. They succeeded. We toured the town on foot, which took less than one hour, during which time we climbed many stairs and ascended to the top of a tower, overlooking this small, old Italian town with its stone-built homes and tiny piazzas. It was picture perfect—with mountains surrounding the town, covered in snow. I witnessed a group of older men sitting in the town square, playing cards, and a group of women outside the bakery, discussing the events of the day. No one hurried anywhere. I don't know where they would have hurried to…though I was completely conscious of feeling rested. As we ambled back to their home, the family friends asked me questions about my family, where I lived, what it is like to be in America. I think it was fun for them to ask me if what they saw on TV is real or not, and to ask what I thought about this topic or that. There have been few times in my life when I felt so welcome by people that I had no connection to, other than the fact that we were sharing a bit of our time together.

Back to pranzo (lunch)…Three "first plates" of pasta. Not one plate with three things on it. No. There were three different, large, full plates of pasta. First was the ravioli, then taglione with fungi, followed by the best lasagna I have ever tasted. I thought, "Well, maybe they are vegetarian or something, so we won't have a meat course." Wrong again. Roasted pork tenderloin, followed by Italian sausages. At this point, we were all stuffed. We took a 45-minute break to go for a walk and try to get the food to move around and make room for more. WHY?? I was clearly the object of everyone's attention—would I, the American, be able to eat my share? It was my job to eat as much as I could, so that I would not offend. Marianna's 11 year-old sister was eating all of it, so I had to keep up…

After the break in the middle of lunch, we returned for the vegetable course—potatoes, green beans, salad, and roasted peppers. Oh my. I was hurting. Next came dessert—mixed fruits with homemade whipped cream. I thought I would just blow up right there. Then there was the dessert cake, and the after dinner café. The men were having after dinner liquors. I was asked to join them, and part of me wanted to—with the women in the kitchen doing the dishes, I was eager to break some stereotypes here. Alas, my stomach couldn't do it. I have no doubt I would have thrown up. Lunch lasted 4 ½ hours, counting the mid-lunch walk. We didn't eat dinner that night, or breakfast the next morning. I wasn't even ready by noon the next day to take another bite.

The Italian music scene—a night at the pub

I have been in search of interesting live music in Italy. Most of what I have found has been bands doing cover songs in English, with strong accents and often not getting the words right. I wanted to hear the real thing! The few Italian gigs I have seen have been one-man shows, a guy singing and playing acoustic guitar. Those have been great, though hard to come by in the center of Rome, where tourists frequent and often request songs from their homeland. I don't understand this, but it truly is what happens.

On Saturday night, though, I went to a pub with a group of Italians to hear live Italian music. What an experience! It was interesting and unlike anything I have heard before. It was a "rock" bank, with an electric guitar, a bass, drums, and a saxophone player who was skilled and attractive (and he knew it). The music itself felt somewhat Spanish or Latin at times, and Scandinavian at others—whatever that might mean. The scene was interesting as well, a mix of ages and dress styles, from the "extremely fancy" to the "more fancy than we were in the U.S, but still casual here" look. People enjoyed the music and cheered and applauded, though they did not dance, and everyone remained seated. Very few people drink to access in Italy—it is largely frowned upon. Each person at our table had one drink, and that was it for the night. We stayed until closing, each of us enjoying the music and the company of the others. So that was what the real thing is all about, huh?

10

The Work I Came to Do

I came to Italy to complete a research project with deaf children and their families. I had no idea what was in store for me when I arrived. Not only was I given a desk at which to work, but officemates with whom to share my experiences, and a research assistant who served as my "right hand woman" and as a good friend throughout my time in Italy. I feel fortunate to have gained so much knowledge from my time there, from the mentors who sponsored me, the professionals with whom I interacted, and the deaf children and their parents, who opened the Italian Deaf World to me for my work. Thank you to each of them.

International Experiences

In my first two weeks here, I have had more "international experiences" than I would normally have in a year. Penny Boyes Braem was here from Austria, and gave a fascinating workshop on the research that she is doing with Swiss German Sign Language. Folks came from all over Europe to attend this function, which was sponsored by the research team with which I am working. I had the chance to attend a workshop during the day with my team. There were 7 of us in total—speaking 4 different languages and using 3 Signed Languages. All of a sudden, more people know ASL than English, so that is becoming my "1st language for communication"—because I know it better than I know Italian. During the same week, Dennis Cokely was here, from the U.S., to do a training on Evaluation of Signed Languages. He was actually here for the whole week, training interpreters, but I only attended the one-day seminar. I met deaf teachers from all over Italy that day, who are teaching LIS to both deaf children and hearing adults. I was stuck by both how similar the Italian deaf community is to that in the U.S., and then struck later in the same day by how different they seemed. They had a lot of patience, and we were able to communicate fairly well. My LIS classes seem to be paying off, and my office mate continues to teach me and challenge me to learn LIS.

Just yesterday, a woman worked with our group who is from Denmark. She has completed a study on group of people in Mexico, the Sarabtek, who have a vocal language, but not a written one. She lived with this group for a year and a half and came to our center for assistance and ideas on how to evaluate the gestural components of their language. The Sarabtek don't use prepositions (e.g. on, under, above)—but rather, they label the parts of the body and "humanize" objects. For example, water being poured into a glass would be "glass stomach" and a book placed on a table would be "face table." Fascinating—and it seems the children learning this language have a far greater spatial capacity at a much younger age. There were people attending yesterday from Norway and Sweden as well.

I am working here, really

Contrary to what you might think if you based your impressions of my time in Rome solely on the stories I have written about my travels here, I really am working. I am doing a research project, or rather a couple of them. I go to the office nearly every workday, though my time there is flexible. I don't have a time to be at work, or a time to leave, so I go when I am in the mood and leave when I am ready. I really like this style of working. It suits me well. I also find that I get a lot done. I don't have to make my work "last" until 5pm, I can instead work diligently to get it done, and when I am finished with what I needed to do for the day at 3:30 or 4pm, then I am rewarded with going home, or going exploring, or having a café' at the bar on the corner. I make time for myself in the morning to go running, do errands, and enjoy watching the sunrise and cast away the shadows on the face of the Chiesa di Santa Maria Maggiore—the magnificent basilica two blocks from where I live. Lately, I have been walking to work. I arrive between 9:30 and 10am. My office is quite large, and I share it with 2 other people—though we each have our own desks and plenty of space—and there are no "dividers" so it is very open. Our ceiling is probably 20 feet high, granting us an amazing window that stretches from floor to ceiling and provides light, air, breeze, and a great view of the sky to our work environment.

My project is coming along. I have spent time translating all of the materials that I used in my dissertation into Italian. This is harder than you might think—I have learned that I am much better at creating phrases in Italian than I am at translating English phrases because the grammar, the tense, and the way that one might pose a question are different. There is no Italian word for "parenting"—which is actually the topic of my study. In discourse with my advisors here, we opted to go with "essere genitore" (to be a parent)—which, in lay terms might seem to be the same, but when you are studying a phenomenon such as the cultural differences between parenting deaf children in America and Italy, asking what it is like to be a parent is different than asking them to describe their parenting processes.

I have a lot of support available to me. I have been assigned an assistant, who will accompany me on my visits to families to conduct interviews, and will help with transcribing the audiotaped interviews into written Italian. She is wonderful, a great person to work with—very intelligent and kind—and she seems genuinely interested in the project. She is working at the CNR as her internship for her master's degree in psychology. There are two other students also completing their "stage" and they are available to assist me whenever I need it as well. The resource library has everything ever written about deafness. I am the resident "expert" in English, and have the opportunity to interact regularly with the director who comes to me and asks me to proofread various letters and proposals that she is sending off to the U.S. for publication. It is fun to be an expert in something, even if it is only my Native Tongue. I have been asked to review a book on deafness for publication, which I happily agreed to do. Being in this place at this time has certainly opened doors for me.

One of the students working at the CNR has been studying English, so I speak to her in Italian and she talks to me in English, and we correct each other when necessary. Recently she asked me, while we were heading out to have lunch together, "Where do you want *to go at for lunch*?" This was such a perfect example of the errors that I make in Italian—the prepositions are different! It is great to talk with folks in Italian who are fluent and can serve as models for my ear, but it is also wonderful to talk with someone learning English so that I am more aware of the errors that I make in learning this new language. In Italian "a" means "in," "at," "to," and "for" depending on the context. My vocabulary is OK—this is where my troubles lie!

At the end of this week, I will be doing my first interview in the home of an Italian family with a deaf child. My Italian Sign Language (LIS) is at the point where I can use it and communicate effectively, so I welcome the chance to chat again with some deaf children. I have missed that. I am very excited to get in there and do this work, to see what I can of their experiences, and to learn all that I am able about "to be a parent" of a deaf child in Italy.

In the homes of the Italian families

I have been doing interviews with Italian families with deaf children for the past couple of weeks. It is exciting to be deeply involved in my research and making huge strides toward its completion. The children are adorable, and I really like having the chance to interact with deaf children in Italy. I hadn't realized how much I missed it until I started working with them again and spending time with them.

In the homes of these families, I have been treated with much respect and the parents have all stated that they are happy to help with research involving deafness because they didn't know anything about it when their children were first diagnosed. There is a strong oralist movement in Italy, nearly all deaf children attend speech therapy and learn to speak. The parents seem to declare their "success" with their deaf child on whether or not the child speaks well, even if they are using sign language methods. It has been interesting for me to note the contrasts here between the deaf people I have met that are Italian and those that I knew from Gallaudet. I am also noting my own biases, thoughts and perceptions on what it means to be deaf. I am constantly amazed at how much I can learn if I just watch and pay attention.

One family had me over for Sunday dinner. It was huge—all of the courses, and we ate for 3 hours. I don't think I have ever been so full in my life, not even on Thanksgiving "unbutton your pants so you can breathe" Day. I was full after the pasta (and they bring that first!). It was great, though, to see this family interact and to feel as though I was a part of it. I truly enjoyed that entire day, and spent time with both children (one deaf, one hearing) playing games in the living room. I felt very fortunate, I think that this was one experience that many Americans traveling abroad would not likely have.

One very special deaf boy

I will call him Matteo. He is a 12 year-old, though he appears to be about eight. He is cute and charming, with a brilliant smile, and a shy grin. He is deaf and has been since birth.

I walked into Matteo's home to interview his mother. I didn't know whether he communicated with sign or speech, as I had not met him prior. I went with the safest route, and said, "Ciao, Matteo" while I did the hand movement that means "ciao" to the deaf. Matteo seemed so eager to talk to me, he was signing away, so quickly that I had to interrupt him and tell him that I am still learning

LIS, but that I want to understand him, and I asked him if he could slow down a little bit for me. He eagerly agreed, and thereafter looked at me after each statement he made, as if to say, "Did you get that?" "What a neat kid," I thought, "so expressive and eager to communicate."

After a few minutes of chatting with Matteo, his mother appeared from the kitchen. She noted his signing and frowned. "Oh no," I thought, "she doesn't want him to sign, and I have been signing with him since I arrived." This mother excused Matteo to his room and asked me to join her in the living room. She seemed a bit irritated. Not a great way to start this interview...

Immediately the mother asked my opinion of signed languages, oral approaches, cochlear implants, and educational opportunities. Yikes, this was supposed to be an interview about her, but clearly she was upset with me, and I needed to clarify my stance and what I intended to do with this research. Although my assistant was with me, every question was directed at me. I needed to answer.

The mother seemed OK with my responses, and seemed to "warm" a little. She told me that her son is being raised orally, and that she and her husband disapprove of the way deaf people look when they sign to each other. She didn't want her son to be "different," she wanted him to speech, and she had paid a lot of money for him to learn to do so. After she defended her position, the mother appeared to let down her guard. She talked openly about her frustrations in dealing with the medical system, and the audiologists. She talked of her deep desire for her son to have close friends, and shared her worry that his deafness would prevent others for seeking his friendship. She laughed and she cried, and I listened as she told the story of the life of her family. The 45 minutes typically scheduled for the interviews turned into 2 hours, and then I left. She hugged me good-bye and stated that she was glad I would be returning in a week for the observation.

As I walked away from the apartment building, I looked up to see Matteo. He was signing out the window and asking me when I was coming back. I looked to see if the mother was looking out the other window, and noted that she wasn't. I signed to him that I would be back the next week and was looking forward to seeing him again. As I got into the car, I felt guilty for signing to him against his mother's wishes, and frustrated that I couldn't communicate with him any other way. Matteo's speech is great, but even with hearing aids, he can't hear me speak, he hears only noises. I spent the entire rest of the day pondering the interview. It was intense. I was trying to "check-in" and see if my reactions were based on a bias against the oral approach, and kept reminding myself that the culture here is different. There is far less access to interpreters and there is no closed captioning, so it may be more important for a deaf person in Italy to speak or read-lips. But Matteo looked defeated when he was sent to his room. I couldn't get that out of my mind.

The next week I arrived for the observation. Matteo greeted me at the door, looked around to see if his mother was watching, and began signing to me—telling me about his day and the new student that came to his school—who is deaf! Matteo signed, "He knows LIS, and said he could teach me more. I hope we become good friends."

Matteo's mother rounded the corner, and I stopped signing. She looked at me and told me to continue. Feeling uncomfortable and unsure, I proceeded signing with Matteo. He looked at his mother in disbelief. She motioned "go on." It was as if he had been given permission to communicate. Matteo signed quickly, telling me everything he could think of, using all of the signs that he knew and had taught himself from a book on sign language that he checked out from his school library. I went into Matteo's room, and looked at the pictures on his walls, as he told me stories about various places and about his friends. He asked me signs, and I was able to teach him a few new ones, which made him smile. This young guy seemed extremely happy. I was happy to be with him.

After I had seen all of the pictures in his room, his collection of soccer player cards, his fish tank, and his computer, I joined Matteo's mother in the living room. With tears in her eyes, she told me how she had watched him communicate with me the week before, and that seeing her son communicate so freely had made a strong impression on her. Over the course of the week, she and her husband had concluded that Matteo needed to communicate, and that signing seemed the most natural way for him to do this. They hadn't told Matteo of their decision, they first wanted to share with me that seeing me sign with their son had changed the way they viewed sign language. It no longer seemed gross to them, but seemed a natural method of expression. Matteo was good at it, having taught himself from a book, he was able to really use this language to communicate his emotions, his thoughts—what was going on inside him.

Oralism works for some deaf children. I cannot deny that it can be extremely beneficial to learn to lip-read, to "fit in" to the hearing world. Cued speech works well for others. Some children can wear hearing aids and correct their hearing to normal levels. This child had used those methods and they worked for him, to a degree. However, given the chance to express himself with his hands, he felt free. I am not sure what will come of my research here—a presentation for sure, possibly a journal article…but I helped one family learn to communicate with each other. Whatever else may come of my time in Italy, I truly believe I was able to assist in making a difference in the life of this child.

As I left, Matteo again appeared at his bedroom window. With pride, he signed "Ciao! Arrevederci!" I signed back, "Ciao, Matteo!" With his hands, Matteo then said, "You have helped me. Thank you." His shy grin had become a broad smile. You have helped me too, Matteo. Grazie mille.

Presentation of my work in Italy

My advisor approached me last week and said that she would like me to do a small presentation for the people at work on the findings of my research before I left. Great. Then we started looking at dates and times, and the best time for everyone was May 8th. Ouch, that was a bit sooner than I had hoped, since my data had not yet all been transcribed, and I had done very little analyses. *OK, I can do this.* "Sure," I say, "That will work." *I have done it now, what have I committed to?* I worked hard on the transcripts in the evenings, and on the analyses during the day. My advisor came in the day before to tell me that she had sent out an email to the rest of the CNR. People from outside our office would be coming to the presentation as well. This was no longer going to be a small, informal group presentation, but something much bigger. *Oh my goodness, this is like a dissertation defense all over again!* I can do this. I have done it before. I know this information and I am comfortable talking about it. *Except maybe not comfortable doing it in Italian...*

The day before the presentation, Marianna and I sat down and organized how we were going to present this information, what categories we had come up with, and who would be presenting which aspects of this work. We worked on the PowerPoint presentation, I did the rough draft in English, and she helped to translate it into accurate Italian. We were feeling good about ourselves at this point, and then she tried to save the presentation to a disc.

My computer died. We didn't know why. It went blank. The screen was dark. It wouldn't turn on, wouldn't turn off, wouldn't do anything—and it was very hot. *Insert your own curse words here, I mean, I probably shouldn't write them, and I didn't say them out loud, but chances are that I thought them.* All of the information was on my computer. I couldn't access it. The presentation was the next day. We worked on some other things, waiting for the computer to "rest." *Heck, what are our other options, right?* None of the other computers in the office have PowerPoint. Marianna and I went home early, and decided to meet early the next morning to proceed and do whatever we needed to next. At that point, we were just walking around in a bit of a daze. *OK—the presentation isn't until 2pm tomor-row; we have time, almost 22 hours in fact. The countdown begins. Crap.*

I did other things when I got home—the dishes, cleaning up, went for a walk…anything but to think about this presentation and my computer. My mood—well, wasn't great. *Did this have to happen today? Why not the day after my presentation instead of the day before? Crap.* At 10pm, I tried my computer again. It worked!!! I couldn't believe it, but I also didn't trust it. I worked on the Power-Point presentation for a few hours, teaching myself how to insert tables and graphs and along the way. *Why is it that I have to re-learn this stuff each time I do a presentation?* I slept for a couple of hours, and then awoke early to meet Marianna at the office. The big day had arrived.

We had a productive morning. We finished the slide presentation. *I hate doing things at the last minute. This is not my style, and it feels icky to me to be under this time pressure.* OK, now, we needed to print the handouts and make copies for the whole group of them. At 12:35-ish we took a quick break for lunch, returned in about 35 minutes, and went to set up the room for the talk at 2pm. Stefano, the tech guy, was there and is ready to help with this process. He had the projector ready. I brought in my laptop and he hooked it up. Nothing. *OK, great. My computer is on the blink again. Fine, we will use another one. At least now everything is saved on a disc, on 3 of them actually.* Marianna brought in her laptop. It didn't work either. The screen on the wall simply said,"No Signal." *This is not good. I don't like this one bit.* The time was 1:50pm. I went to my CNR advisor, and asked to use her laptop. Stefano was working away on getting this set up. People had arrived, and the room was filling up. My co-workers, one-by-one, learned what had happened. They asked me, in turn, "Are you OK? Are you freaking out?" *Why are you asking me that? Why? I am sure it is out of the goodness of your heart, but it makes me want to throw something right now.* The time is 2:10pm. Those questions were followed by, "You are so calm. I can't believe you are han-dling this so well." *What is my option, really? I have to do this whether I have the slides or not. I look calm on the outside but inside I am thinking crap, crap, crap!* I began to make overheads of the presentation. I printed the first couple of pages on overhead sheets, and then the printer jammed. *Of course the printer just jammed. Is this what they refer to when they site Murphy's law? Bad luck? Crap.* The time was 2:15pm. *I was going to make overheads earlier, and was told they didn't have many extra overhead sheets. I should have listened to my instincts…crap. There are many deaf folks in the audience. I really need to have visual things to help them follow, especially with my Italian…crap—I have to do this in Italian. Almost, in some way, had forgotten about that.* The time is 2:20pm, and the "audience" is in place. Luckily, this is Italy, so starting late is normal....

Stefano yelled down the hall that it was working. He had gotten the projector to work, it was hooked up to a laptop, and the presentation was ready. *Here goes....*

It went well. Amazingly, I think the presentation was OK. My Italian was, of course, a bit shaky. *But 6 months ago, I didn't know any Italian. I am doing a presentation on my research to my colleagues and peers in Italian. This is neat.* At some point, shortly after the beginning, when the immediacy of the recent events wore away, this began to be fun. The audience seemed to "get it," they asked good questions and were interested in the topic. The interpreter did a great job. He only stopped me once and asked for clarification, the rest of the time he did an amazing job of changing my sometimes-incorrect pronunciations or grammatical slip-ups. *I have to remember that the pronoun comes before the verb…and remember to change tenses when comparing past research done by others with current research done by u…and remember to…*

At the end of the presentation, I gave Marianna flowers to thank her for her assistance with this project. She has been great, and has gone above and beyond the call of duty in terms of the work that she needed to do. *I can't believe we just finished this presentation. My time in Italy is actually coming to an end…*Marianna got tears in her eyes, turned bright red, and stepped away quickly, out of the limelight. My Fulbright advisor was there, and she said a few words at the end as well, thanking the CNR for hosting me, and sharing the story of my selection for the Fulbright award. Apparently, they thought my credentials were good, but they thought my proposal was impossible. I was proposing to complete a study in 4 months that the 9 months Fulbright students do not finish. I wanted to interview parents in Italian, and at the time of writing my proposal, I had not learned a single word of Italian, had never had a class. They called me back in the late summer to see if I really thought this would be possible in the length of time that I was in Italy. I told them I could do it. They believed me. Or maybe they just decided to take a chance on me…

Celebrating under the stars

I met up with Marisa and Diane to celebrate the completion of my project. We went to an art opening (Diane is a printmaker, and knows many artists in Rome) at the American Academy of Rome, and saw some amazing pieces by an artist who paints objects that look like they are in motion. The American Academy is gorgeous, on the largest hill in Rome, across the river. The studio was on the top floor, and the small gathering that was held afterward was on a rooftop deck overlooking the city. It was a gorgeous evening; we saw the sunset in the distance. We ordered pizza and ate outside. I met some interesting people, from all over, doing fascinating things. None of us were from Rome, but life had brought us here at the same time. It was a nice night—a mellow way to celebrate and relax after a long couple of days. Just what the doctor ordered.

11

The People in Italy who Touched My Heart

The homeless man down the street

Every day I walk by a homeless man on my way to catch the bus or the metro. Every day. A couple of days ago, I was moved to tears by this situation, and I was not sure what to do about it or how to change it. At first I was afraid—this man is large, smells bad, and I did not want to go near him. I have noticed this is also the approach that others have taken…they walk by without looking down and don't seem to know that he is there. Every day.

I know homelessness is not unique to Rome in any way, though I don't think I have been confronted with it in quite the same way ever before in my life. A couple weeks ago I decided to brave it and try to talk to this man. How do you address a man that lives on the street? Italian uses an informal and a formal tense. Surely I should use the formal tense, since I don't know this man, and he is obviously older than I am. Has he ever been addressed that way before? I spoke to him and he said nothing, he did not look up at me and did not acknowledge my existence. Do you suppose that is learned behavior?

Being my brave self, on my way home that evening I again spoke to this homeless man. He looked at me, but didn't speak and did not give any outward signs of comprehension. Might he be deaf? OK—I know I tend to overestimate that prevalence, but I am learning LIS and might be able to…so I signed to him while I spoke and he said nothing.

The next day, it was raining quite hard. I have two umbrellas, one good one and one that is much smaller, that I had bought on my previous trip to Italy when I forgot to bring mine. I gave him the smaller of the two. I handed the homeless man the umbrella, and he did not take it from my hands. I set it beside this man, who sits on an old blanket, against a wall. That is where he always sits. Every day.

A few days later, as I approached him, I thought to myself, "Why did I keep the large one for myself?" I questioned my motives all day long. Had I not had an extra, would I have purchased one for this man? If I was honest with myself and said, "Probably not"—then I would have to face the facts that I am selfish enough to not spend 3 euro on a man without a home. Shouldn't I share the best of what I have in material things with this man, since I do have a roof over my head and a place to shower, and food to eat, and clothes to cover me?

Despite my false bravery, I did not know how close I wanted to get. You know the stories, right—"young woman is beaten by homeless man..." However, the moment I imagined others not wanting to be close to me, to be afraid to touch me, that was the first time that this gentleman really touched my heart. I love hugs. Some people in my family call me "The hugger."—I enjoy close relationships with friends and family and believe strongly in showing affection and telling people that I care about them. What if I had no one to hug, no one to hug me back, and people were afraid of me and didn't want to be near me? I felt sad.

The homeless man is a constant presence in my world. Not a day passes that I don't pass him. I have certainly considered the possibility that he is mentally ill—again, something I am likely to overestimate, given my line of work, but...The thought that he might be mentally ill bothers me and gives me comfort at the same time. I don't know where to point him for resources, medications, shelters, or food. I also don't know that he wants that. The comfort comes from the fact that his mind may be busy, and may not ponder his existence in the same way that mine does. I hope that is true.

Today, for the first time, the gentleman was using the umbrella that I had given him, the small one that I don't like as well. I wanted to trade him and apologize for not being more considerate sooner. Every day I will continue to wonder what I can and should do about him, for him. Every day I hope that I won't see him there on the sidewalk, next the wall, close to the garbage cans. Every day. Yet today was different, as I walked by, he smiled. And I smiled back.

Antonio

I was walking on the street, heading home late in the afternoon, carrying an extra bag with the new dictionary I had just purchased, and not thinking much of anything when I saw him. He was gorgeous. Probably the cutest 3 year-old I have ever seen. He had dark wavy hair, and an almond complexion. His eyes were large and wide, deep brown like a fine polished wood. I noticed him and smiled immediately. How adorable he was! He walked right up to me, smiling and showing the dimple on his left cheek, and said, "Mi chiamo Antonio." "Ciao, Antonio!" I said. To that he responded, "Ciao, Bella." Antonio is learning early how to be a charmer! I had to resist my urge to hug him. Little Antonio grabbed my hand, innocently and without thought it seemed. He and I were going to walk together.

At that instant I thought of Antonio's mother. I looked around and saw no one paying particular attention to me or to this beautiful little boy. Given Antonio's charm and "comfortability with strangers," I immediately assumed that he had wondered off. That was probably a trait his mother despised, I thought, and I wondered if Antonio was aware of his surroundings. With his hand still in mine, we approached the street corner. I anticipated seeing an Italian woman, with her hands on her head, saying, "Oh mio Dio!" (Oh my God)—a phrase so commonly heard here that I couldn't imagine anything else being said in its place.

What I did see was something so much worse. I saw a woman sitting on the ground, a baby in her lap and a sign asking for money. Antonio looked up at me, with his deep, dark eyes. He just kept looking at me, staring. His eyes the color of chestnut wood were penetrating. It felt as though he were looking into me rather that at me. I asked him what was wrong. He said, "Niente" (Nothing.) He squeezed my hand hard—harder than I thought would be possible coming from this little 3 year-old body. I was still looking for his mother, glancing down the street to see if I could see a woman who looked like she was looking for her son. Apparently she had already found him. I glanced down at Antonio in time to feel the last of his squeeze on my hand, and to see his big smile, showing his dimple. Then he let go of my hand and walked over to the woman on the ground and said, "Mi dispiace, Mamma." (I am sorry, Mama). The woman on the ground, with the baby in her lap, handed Antonio the cup that was to be used to beg for money. Then she took her hands and placed them on either of Antonio's cheeks, and physically turned Antonio's smile into a frown. Gone was his dimple, and gone was the little flicker of spirit that I had seen. My newest little friend was told to turn around and to ask for money, and to not smile like that because then people would not think that he was poor. Antonio, being a good boy, did exactly as his mother told him. He did not say good-bye to me, nor I to him. I think he was afraid to look at me, in much the same way I was afraid to make eye contact with his mother.

Antonio's life will not be easy. It saddens me that life itself might be enough to break him down. It is difficult to imagine his life, and all that goes with it. As I made my way across the street, I imagined Antonio as an 8 year old. Would he be able to go to school? What types of friends will he have, living in this situation? Then I imagined Antonio as a teenager…would he leave his mother and go out on his own? Would he join the other young men living in the park? Would he go on to change the course of his life, to go to school, to work, maybe to have a family someday? As I stood on the corner opposite his post, I looked back and wondered all of these things. "Antonio," I thought to myself but wanted to scream, "You can beat these odds. Don't allow yourself to be broken. Be a fighter, be resilient, and be strong." I so badly wanted to share these thoughts with sweet little Antonio, who had called me "Bella." But he is only 3 years old, would he even understand?

To say that Antonio touched my heart would be an understatement. He touched my soul.

The Italian grandmother

Marianna's grandmother is a cute, old, short, wrinkled, fierce, little woman. She kissed me when she met me, squeezing my cheeks and welcoming me to her home. She speaks in a dialect that was difficult for me to understand, so much of the time I spent trying to figure out what she was saying, or looking to her family to interpret for me into Italian that I understood. I am not talking about an accent here, but a truly different dialect. I was struck, in talking to her, by the fact that the land I was standing on had at various times not been part of the same country as the land I was living on. This area of Italy was different, with its own customs and language.

Like any good grandmother, this little lady encouraged me to eat (she stands about at the height of my shoulder, and I am just 5'2"—if I am standing really tall and wearing shoes). "Manga, seniorina, manga!" She never once called me Amy, preferring instead to call me seniorina, and I referred to her as "seniora"—out of respect.

Marianna's grandmother is a living history of stories. In her 88 years, she has lived a great deal, and she likes to share what she has experienced and what she knows. I love old people. I thoroughly enjoy spending time hearing these stories, gleaning what I can from their experiences. There is something very special in the way an older person tells a story. It is different, I think, than what we usually hear as the recounting of facts in our daily lives. Older people tend to have the time to tell you the details—how they felt about things, what the impact was of the actions they are speaking about. In part, I think this is because older people have earned the right to their opinions. I might think such and such about the depression, or WWII, or some other event in recent history, but they have lived it, so they have a certain sense of knowing that is foreign to me. I miss having older people actively in my life.

When I lived in Kentucky, my landlords, who owned the house that I lived in (my apartment was in the basement) were my educators, and my friends. Homer and Katherine—they have touched my life. He would tell stories of growing up in Kentucky at the turn of the century, a marble for a toy, and that was all. She would share the tale of falling in love with Homer when they both went to college, Katherine spoke of marrying him and moving into the little house owned by the university. They would hold hands while they talked, gently correcting the other for their lapses in memory. That did not matter to me, though, what mattered was their joy in telling their stories, their love in sharing their life together. I cared for them both. I thought of Katherine as I spoke to Seniora, missing her and the times that she shared just like this, only in a different land, a different language. Katherine passed away a few years ago, but I felt her presence throughout that day. I am so lucky to have had her as a part of my life. I had the feeling that the Seniora had that impact on people as well...

I am an early riser, as is the Seniora. While the rest of the family slept, we sat in the kitchen, again, her alternatingly holding my hand, and pinching my cheeks. We discussed the events of her life—the fact that her mother lived in America for a short time, and returned to Italy just in time for her baby to be born. I learned about the children she raised, the husband she lost, and the life she now leads. Seniora cried as she told me the story of her life, pausing for effect and to make sure that I understood her. When my brain would re-order the words she said and make sense of them, I would nod my head, indicating that I understood, and then she would continue. The Seniora spoke lovingly of her children and grandchildren. She scolded me for being so far away from my own mother, and told me I should start working on being a mother myself, since that is what life is about—loving and living, and creating life, in her words. She countered this by saying that she was proud that I was not rushing off to get married, and that she admired the fact that I wanted to travel and see the world before I "settled down." We drank espressos with milk and ate leftover Easter bread as we shared the stories of our lives. Holding hands, I felt a connection to this Italian woman that I will cherish long after I forget the details of our discourse.

Another Special Little Boy

Cristina, my friend and colleague from Brazil, invited me to spend the day with her family to celebrate the "Day of the Worker" as it is called in Brazil. I awoke early and met them at the train station to head out for a day in the country.

It was a treat to meet her family. I have been hearing about them so much and had seen many pictures. I felt like I knew them before I actually saw them in person. I knew that her husband works as an industrial engineer, and that they have been married for 15 years. They met as teenagers, protesting the political activities of their Brazilian government. I knew from Cristina's stories that her daughter, Anna, was 11 years-old, and had been getting many calls from the boys at her school. She was developing quickly, and is simultaneously a young girl and an almost teenager. I also know that Giovani, her 8 year-old son, had been having some difficulties in school. He had some motor integration problems that have caused other children to tease him, to not accept him. He also had an attentional problem that prohibits him from sitting still for longer than a few seconds. He is not of those overmedicated children with ADHD—his attentional difficulties are real. His teachers have had several meetings with Cristina, telling her that they do not know how to work with her son. In a rare moment of allowing herself to feel sad, Cristina and I had shared tears in the park for Giovani. As his mother, she couldn't bear to hear the words his teachers had told her, "Your son is bad," "He can't behave," "We don't want him in our school," and, "Maybe your son would be better off if you home-schooled him." As her friend, I shared her sorrow and my heart went out to her.

Anna greeted me first; in a very grown-up posture she shook my hand while she said, "Piacere. Mi chiamo Anna." I received kisses on either cheek from Cristina's husband, a handshake, and a "Piacere." Giovani peeked out from behind his father, looked up at me, and said, "Hi. Nice to meet you. My name is John." Perfect English. I tried to keep my jaw from dropping while I shook his hand and said, "My name is Amy. Nice to meet you." He beamed, and stepped in front of his father, ready to interact with this stranger who was joining them for day.

Once we boarded the train for Frasceti, Giovani alternated between his mother's lap, the floor, the seat next to his sister, his father's lap, the walkway, and finally, half on my lap, and half on the seat next to me, sprawled out like a mummy, pretending, for about five seconds, that he was dead. Then, he looked at me and said, "Merci baucoup." "Tu conosce Francese? (Do you know French?)" He smiled widely. Next, Giovani told me the words that he knows in Spanish, German, French and English. His native language is Portuguese, and in the four months that he has lived here, he has become nearly fluent in Italian. "Smart kid," I thought to myself, "I hope he knows that he is bright."

I was astonished with Giovanni's parents. They both impressed me with their patience and dedication to this child. Other parents on the train were telling their children to "sit up straight" and "don't talk to adults"—these parents seemed to accept Giovani and his behaviors. They did ask him to move when the others needed to use the walkway, but they accepted his fitfulness with such normality. They took pleasure in the things that he knows, and hugged him frequently. There is no doubt that this child is loved completely and that he knows he is loved. I knew intuitively that Cristina was a good mother. One can tell in the way that she shares the stories of her children, the way that her head tilts and she forms a small smile while describing the events of her life with her family. She is able to put herself in her son's position and seems to understand him so well. Giovanni's father, also, celebrates his son and the interesting aspects that arise from raising a child like Giovani. As they looked out the window at the Roman Aqueduct, Giovani half-listened while his father described the old water system, as he wiggled around and tried to kick the seat opposite him to see if he could reach. At the conclusion of this description, Giovani grabbed his father's face in his small hands and said, "I love you, Dad" in Portuguese. "I love you too, Son."

We arrived, the five of us, in Frasceti, at 10am. We set off for a hike through gorgeous terrain, gradually climbing to an old Roman theatre, and reached a park on top of a large hill that overlooks a large lake, a couple of castles, and the quaint little city below. Giovani held my hand as we began our ascent. In Italian, he described his school in Brazil. He was surprised when he asked me if I knew the name of the president of Brazil, and I did. Admittedly, this is because of the recent election there, where the new president, Mr. Lulu, is the first left-winged ruler in many years—and because I share an office with Cristina. He told me, "In school they only teach us about Italy. I tell them about Brazil all the time." I had no doubt that was true. As we walked, I learned more about Brazilian food, Brazilian soccer, and Brazilian geography. Giovani is a good teacher. All of a sudden, he let go of my hand, and off he went. He ran up ahead, taking his mother with him. I thought nothing of this, being his nature, until I rounded a corner and saw Giovani standing there, a bouquet of wild flowers in his hand, looking at me with a large grin on his face, "Per te (For you)." I bent down to take the flowers and he hugged me. I hugged back and felt the tears burning behind my eyes. I was so touched by this young heart, so pure and uninhibited, so spontaneous and loving.

I recalled, at that moment, the words of his mother—the frustrations of his physical therapist, the teasing of his classmates, the discouragement from his teachers. Why is the world so mean? Why do we want everyone to be the same? Could those people not see the specialness exuding from this little boy? Will he know, does he know, that he brings people joy?

Our walk was lovely, a gradual winding up the hill, with a great vista at the top. We shared a picnic lunch and ran around with the other picnickers on the grass at the top. There were several families, and groups of young people, since it was a day off for most of Italy. Giovani was tired, he said, and he needed to rest. His "rest" lasted for about four bites of food, and then he was off to explore, because he thought he saw a frog. He was definitely a "boy," no doubt about that. After lunch, we continued our hike and explored the upper part of the plateau before heading back down to the town. Along the way, Giovani stopped us all to look at a group of butterflies that he had discovered. We played the "animal game" where we went through the alphabet and thought of the name of an animal for each letter—first in Italian, then in English. Anna was the best at this game, having had several years of English lessons in her school in Brazil.

The gelato we ate in town was great, some of the best I have had. Giovani spilled it down the front of his shirt, and his parents giggled a bit and helped him clean it up. There was no yelling at him for being too active, only acceptance that this is the way he was, and an appreciation for his sense of humor when these things happen. He doesn't get angry or frustrated, he just gives a look, which is quite cute, I have to say. It seemed to indicate, "Oops. Can you believe what happened this time?" The contrast was provided for me by the father sitting opposite us on the other bench, yelling at his 3 year-old for letting the gelato drip onto her dress.

I think Giovani is fortunate to have the parents that he has. I do not know many parents that would handle this situation with such grace, courage, and compassion. I do not think, though, that Giovani is a "lucky kid." He has many challenges to face, obstacles to overcome. I hope, wish, and pray, that he can maintain his sense of self, his humor, and his strong character. I hope that his teachers in the future, and the children that will interact with him, will see his incredible strengths. In seeing this adorable child, and in knowing a bit of his story, I can't help but feel both saddened by the constricting nature of society, in trying to shape every child to fit into a perfect mold, and encouraged by the fact that there are people like Giovani in the world, teaching us lessons about what is really important. Maybe his purpose in life is to remind us that following the rules, sitting still, and raising your hand before you speak are not the most important aspects there are to being human. Maybe it is more important that we share what we feel, tell people we care about them, pick flowers for our friends, and stop to really see the butterflies and marvel at their beauty.

The convent

A couple of weeks ago, just before I went on vacation, I had the opportunity to go with Marianna to go to her old place of work—a convent that houses deaf adolescents. It was an interesting and unique experience, one that changed the way that I see things. Yet another one of those experiences...

The girls are between the ages of 12 and 23, and they live in the convent with the nuns. They attend a regular school, then return each day to the "dorms." In my mind's eye, I had pictured a "convent" as being old and run-down. Instead, this was a gorgeous building, with large windows overlooking a beautifully kept garden. In the not-so-distant past this building, with its 4 floors and 2 wings, was full of deaf students. Now, only one wing on one floor is used to house the "ragazze"—the rest is empty. As in the United States, there has been a significant push in Italy to mainstream deaf children in the classrooms with deaf children. The numbers are dwindling, and the nuns are concerned that they may not be enough students to keep the facility open next year. The students that remain, the majority of them anyway, have other disabilities in addition to their deafness. The families of these girls live in remote parts of Italy, so this is their one opportunity to attend school and to be with other deaf children.

I had the opportunity to practice some of the Italian Sign that I have been learning. The girls were readily impressed that I had come to Italy and had learned a bit of LIS. I was so glad that I had taken the time to work on that, even if I do not use it much in my future, but then again, who knows? They asked many questions about America, eagerly wanting to know what it is like to live in Washington, DC, what the fashions are like in the U.S., and what deaf teens there are doing. Do they live in residential facilities? Do they live with their parents? Do they date other deaf people? Actually, there were many, many questions about dating. They were teenage girls, after all...

One of the neatest things in the whole wide world is seeing someone in his or her element. Seeing an artist create a masterpiece before your very eyes, or watching an athlete excel for the pure sport of it, or a teacher who gets through to a child—these things give meaning to life. Marianna is in her element when she interacts with deaf children. They adore her. She understands them and has such a wonderful relationship with them that even someone without any knowledge of sign language could readily see it. They eagerly await her arrival, and each, in turn, talks to her. They share what is happening at school, what is happening with the other girls on the floor, what is happening with this boy that they like, or that girl that they don't. She is for them a sounding board, a counselor of sorts, and a trusted adult that many of them do not have in their lives. Marianna is not judgmental of them, and they know this, in witnessing their interactions, you can see trust and respect, on both ends.

The nuns that run this convent for the deaf do not know sign language. They rely on the assistants that work there to interact with the children. Some of them read lips, others are learning to fingerspell, but none can communicate fluently with this girls. New assistants that work there now, and Marianna just comes to visit, to see "the girls" that she has grown to care so much about. The other assistants can communicate with the children, but with Marianna it is different. This is her element. In watching her, you know that this is what she is supposed to be doing with her life. I felt fortunate to be a part of this interaction, and lucky to have a friend who is so special to so many.

12

Implications of Living a Simple Life

Living in America, it is easy to forget that other countries, and other people, do not have the same privileges that we do. Living abroad has taught me that the "American perspective" is one perspective, but not the only one. I recognize that being in Italy is not like being in a third world country. I am not trying to draw that comparison, though I would like to encourage my fellow Americans to step outside of our large country and try to see the world from the perspective of one of the "little guys"—countries not quite so powerful as our own. The actions that we take and the ways in which we live our lives are not simply our "choice," they are real actions with real consequences that have far-reaching impacts on the world.

Bowling for Columbine

I saw the movie "Bowling for Columbine" at a theater here in Rome. If you haven't seen it, I highly suggest it. It is a documentary by Michael Moore, and gives some interesting insights and perspectives into American culture, particular the violence in our society.

Italians don't observe the unwritten American rule that you should not sit directly next to someone you don't know in a movie theater. So…this Italian guy sat right next to me and watched this movie. At the intermission, he asked me if I was American, and I said that I was. He said, "This is scary, doesn't it scare you?" This comment was in response to the fact cited that more Americans are murdered (11,000 per year from guns) than in any other country. Canada has about 400 per year, for example, even though a greater percentage of their population has guns and they have more total guns than the U.S. In Detroit in the year 2000, there were more murders than any other U.S. city, but the number of murders in the Canadian town just across the river was zero—in fact, only 2 had occurred in the last 20 years). I don't remember many of the stats now, but I encourage you to see the film if you haven't.

I chatted with this guy again after the film, and was fascinated to get his perspective on violence, on the American media, on the culture of fear, on the "bullying" that happens in America, and the bullying that America does abroad. This guy was very kind. He was accepting of me. He was not belittling Americans, or me but questioned the motives of a government that provokes violence. Regardless of where you stand on the issues of the U.S. in the Middle East, I think it is important to hear some of the perspectives of other countries and other places. It does give fresh insight into the media-lead "cause" and reminds us that we are not alone, and that every action that we take impacts the larger world around us.

Consumerism

My latest read has been "No Logo." The author is Naomi Klein, a Canadian writer who has been labeled "the next Noam Chomsky"—she is liberal, a journalist, and the originator of the No Logo campaign against multi-national corporations. I should preface this by saying that I do own some "name brand" things, and that I do not know what the answers should be to the problems that we face. Here are just some thoughts:

Since Wal-Mart brands and the expensive "name brand" clothing popular in the U.S. are made by the some people in the factories in countries that many of us have never heard of, which is better? Should we "go cheap" and not give our money to the logo-promo people? Can we continue to support Wal-Mart, which now controls ¼ of all retail sales in the States? They pull magazines from their shelves that they don't deem "family quality" and refuse to sell medication such as the "morning after pill," because they are personally against it—fine, but when you are the only store in some towns, and they have no other options for retail shopping because the Wal-Marts of the world have pushed the small business owners out of business and emptied out downtowns and they have created the "shopping mecas" outside of town (thus detracting from the sense of community)—well, maybe that isn't so fine after all. Regardless of your stance on birth control, or on magazines that are not "family-centered," or on rap music with "offensive lyrics"—the fact that they are not available at all, and that a company is deciding what you are permitted the opportunity to buy, that is censorship.

I remember being in Coquille when the Wal-Mart came to Coos Bay, Oregon. I heard talk of how it would send Taylor's Sports out of business, because the prices there were higher than at "Wally World." It did. The impact of this was not only lower priced basketballs for the team, but the loss of a business that was central to that small town. Taylor's had for years sponsored the middle school yearbook, given money for the high school team's rosters, and been a member of the community. It now stands as an empty building in the center of town, a reminder that the town center is disappearing. Sure, Wal-Mart provides jobs. For some people, working part-time, flexible hours is exactly what they want in their lives. For others, the lack of opportunity to work full-time at these stores (they hire for 38 hours a week, so that they do not have to pay for health insurance or other benefits) is detrimental to the quality of life of them and their families. It is very different owning one's own store than it is being a "sales associate" for a major conglomeration.

As a student who has been living on graduate student stipends (which, for the record, do not pay real well) and student loans now for a long time, I understand the desire to buy things "cheap." I get it, really. When you have $12 in your checking account and the cheap version of something costs $10, and the more expensive is $18…well, I understand that people often do what they need to do. I am not in a self-righteous position to condemn, simply in a position to share some thoughts. I believe that we vote with our dollars, and the way we chose to support the businesses around us will dictate how they develop. Maybe, as consumers, we just need to be more aware of the fact that the purchases we make impact our communities, our states, our nation, and the rest of the world. When a "fad" like a new Disney movie comes out and we want to buy the stuffed animals, the t-shirts with the logo, and the Happy Meals with the Disney toys—we need to know that a new factory is set up for that purpose, most likely in Taiwan. Last year's Disney t-shirt sold at Wal-Mart for $10.94—an amount that Taiwan factory workers would need to work for 2 weeks to purchase, working 18 hour days. Yet, each of these workers made over 120 of those t-shirts every day.

I have been an advocate for "independents" for a long time—preferring small stores and cool, interesting coffee shops to the chains. For a long time, I proudly claimed that I had not been to a Starbucks, but alas, now I have, so I know that what I say could be perceived as hypocritical (but only twice…). That is the point though—I am not damning those who own certain items, we all have given into this branding culture, whether we wanted to or not, or whether we were even aware that we were doing it at the time. As a runner, I need running shoes, and I buy new ones usually twice a year. It was disheartening to learn that all of the major brands are made in the same 3 factories—be they Nike, Adidas, or Reeboks—what can I do? It is difficult to even comprehend the influence of the name branding on our lives.

Here is just a bit of what I have learned:

- Tommy Hilfinger does not make anything. *Nothing*. And it never has. It is only a brand. The jeans are made by Pepe jeans, the shirts made by the Gap, and other items are made by different companies that "sublet" the brand. That is why we pay the big bucks.

- The same sweatshop in the Far East that makes clothes for the Gap, also make the Wal-Mart brands, and the clothes sold by Old Navy.

- Michael Jordan's pay for one year for being a "spokesman" for Nike is equivalent to the pay received by all of the sweatshop workers—combined.

- The factory that makes Nike, Adidas, and L.A. Gear don't pay their workers enough to own a pair of the shoes they make. It would cost 6 months to save enough, working 18-hour days.

- The stock options given to the CEO of Disney last year, not including his salary, would have been enough to provide housing, food, and medical care to the 19,000 employees and their families that work in the Disney plant in Haiti—for four whole years.

- Multinational companies have more power than most governments, without the democratic controls in place that provide for the "checks and balances" that we strive to achieve in government. I believe that we need to hold them accountable for the power they wield.

- There is a whole movement afoot for challenging this status quo—via the *Adbusters* magazine and action teams, student groups against sweatshop use, and such groups as the World Social Forum. I am by far not the first to consider the implications of our purchasing dollar, and won't be the last. Groups across the country, and in other countries, are working to collectively inform consumers of the impact of their decisions. Taking back power is empowering.

- The issues of the "Third World" are not just sad stories of groups of people that are far away from us. We can't distance ourselves from them, and shouldn't—first of all because *we are all human*, and secondly because *our actions directly impact them*, regardless of how separate we are being brought to believe we are.

Grocery Shopping

Grocery shopping in Italy is not the chore I once believed it was when I was in the U.S. Going to the grocery, fighting the lines, finding the time to "stock up" on all I might need for the next few weeks—none of these things is pleasant to me. In Italy, I went to the store almost daily. It became a pleasure to see the same faces as I walked home from work and stopped at the fruit stand, where the local grower would willingly teach me the Italian terms for exotic fruits and vegetables. I tasted food for what felt like the first time in Italy. The idea that one would buy something "green" and wait for it to ripen was foreign to these foreigners. Why would you not buy it fresh? When it is ready and ripe and perfect for eating? Good point, really. I believe that by simplifying our lives, experiencing the joy that can be involved in grocery shopping, in talking with those in your community, in taking pride in what you put into your body, and in cherishing shared meals with others, we can simply our lives and find happiness.

13

Italian Celebrations

Carnivale

As those of you familiar with Marti Gras might know—many countries around the world celebrate the "carnival" for the 5 days preceding Ash Wednesday and the start of Lent in the Christian tradition. I have never been to Marti Gras and didn't know what to expect with the "carnivale" in Rome, but I stayed in town for the weekend in order to check out it. I will first tell you about the parade—and then the chocolate!

The parade was smaller than expected, probably due to the rain that poured down all day from the gray skies. It was still festive, fun, and interesting. I saw young children in costumes and face paint, older children with confetti that they threw at every adult within five feet, and grown children on stilts, dancing to the music and acting as mimes. I enjoyed the atmosphere—the carefree spirit of it all. There were several different bands playing, the streets were lined with carnival masks, and fun was being had by all.

And now for the chocolate…My roommate and I went to the Villa Borghese to attend the European chocolate celebration, which was happening in conjunction with the Carnivale. OH MY! There were several hundred vendors, from all over Europe, selling chocolate in various forms—from chocolate pasta (those were made by the Italian vendors, by the way), to chocolates made with beer, to chocolates with hot peppers (as in the movie Chocolat), to chocolate liquor, sauce, and toppings. Hazelnuts are big in Italy, and they abound at this festival—chocolate-covered hazelnuts—one place had them with 12 different kinds of chocolate. We sampled some (until we really didn't want any more chocolate, at all, for at least a year), and we brought some home. Of course, by the next day, that disgusting chocolate overload feeling was gone, and the eating commenced anew.

On Tuesday, at work, co-workers brought the various chocolates that they had purchased, as well as treats from the bakery and even some homemade biscotti. I asked the reason for the festivities as work, and received one of those looks like, "You really don't know? Are you serious?" I was told that I should have as much fun as possible, because the next day the fun would stop and there would be no more festivities for 40 days. Well, I have given up things for Lent before, but I had never seen the graveness of this situation. One co-worker told me, "Really, you can't have any more fun. Or if you do, don't tell anybody, because it is Lent." OK, I promise to keep it a secret....

Liberation Day 2003

I have written before about my experiences in Italy at a time when many Italians had not been in agreement with the political actions of the U.S. Some Americans have expressed concern that Europeans do not remember their actions in both World Wars. Those individuals do not perceive the Europeans as being thankful for their assistance. Here is a story that I want you to hear:

Friday, April 25th was the day that Italy celebrated Liberation Day. This is the day that the Americans assisted Italy and overthrew Mussolini. All over the country, there were American flags, and signs that said, in Italian, "Thank you, America, for helping to free us." This is a major occasion in Italy, celebrated with parades, a day off of work, and talks and presentations to commemorate the overthrowing of a fascist dictator. The leaders of Italy at that time had been in support of Hitler, though by all accounts, the vast majority of the people were not. When the groups within Italy began to resist the Nazi regime, many of them were killed by their own weapons. Since Italy is a peninsula and Germany lies to its north, it was extremely difficult for the Italian people to escape the brutality of the war. I read accounts in the papers and had discussions with Italians on Liberation Day, regarding their feelings upon seeing the American soldiers arrive, with food and supplies and hope. They were grateful and appreciative. They will never forget. I was thanked, as an American, for being willing to help them. I was not alive at that time, but here is to those of you who were...

Buona Prima di Maggio!

Happy 1st of May! What a celebration this is in Italy! May Day, for much of the world, is Labor Day, a day of political activity on behalf of workers. There are parades, speeches, and musical celebrations. Interestingly, I was told that May 1st was a day of protest in the United States at the turn of the century, where a group of workers in Chicago went on strike for worker's rights. I found it interesting that much of the world celebrates this event that occurred in the U.S., though May 1st is not a national holiday there.

Last night I went with a group of four other women to see the festivities and hear the music. The festival was held at St. Giovanni of Laterino. It is about 7-8 blocks from my house, so we met here and headed out on foot to see what "Prima di Maggio" was all about.

There were so many people! The event had been going on since early afternoon, though the partying was certainly picking up as we entered evening. We were not close enough to see the stage, though the large screens provided a good view of the musicians and dancers on stage. Each band played three songs, and then a new band would come to the stage. I witnessed performances by the most popular acts in Italy. The audience was "hooting and hollering" and encouraging each performer. Frederico di Grego sang a song of peace and love that moved the crowd to pull out their lighters and to sway from side to side while hugging their neighbors. Many Italian teenagers had purchased headbands that said, "Prima di Maggio—La festa piu grande in Italia" (May 1st—the biggest party in Italy). The events of the day were broadcast on television throughout Europe. As we walked home, we witnessed the party on the news on the TV in one of the bars.

Between acts, there were short "pep talks" about labor and worker rights, and many songs were tailored to this theme. Once again, I was astonished at the liberal perspectives provided by the Communist Party, so contrary to my childhood notion of Communism. I can't pretend to know the ins-and-outs of their ideology. I do know that they are recognized as the most politically active party in this country, on behalf of the people.

Since there were so many people, there was the unfortunate pushing and shoving that tend to accompany large crowds. Plenty of people who had been there all day, drinking and smoking various substances, and at the point in the evening when we arrived, people were getting sick. After my shoe was thrown up on, I remembered why I don't usually like big crowds. We headed home around midnight, just before the end of the festivities, trying to beat the crowds out of there. Despite the stink on my shoe, I had enjoyed myself and was happy to have been a part of the celebration of the day. May Day has taken on new meaning for me.

Cinco di Mayo

Having told you about May 1st, let me tell you about May 5th. Not quite the same. Linda, Graham and I decided to go out for Mexican food to celebrate Cinco di Mayo. Now, granted, it is difficult to find Mexican restaurants in Italy, but come on—this was a day of celebration! We looked in the phone book and found 2 options. We called them and one was closed. The other had a recording that said it opens every day at 8pm. It was 7:50—we headed out and walked there. It was in an obscure place. We kept following the road, since we hadn't yet reached the address indicated in the phone book, but it didn't seem right, far away, down a dark street. We pressed on.

We found it, and they were closed. On Cinco di mayo!!! We couldn't believe it. What a hoax. By this time, it was well after 9pm, and we were hungry. We ate Italian food, and then went to a bar for a margueritas afterward. Not quite the same though…

14

Life Changes and Struggling to Be Me

On my way to Albuquerque

In March, I found out where I would be placed for my last year of clinical training, my internship. I had applied all around the country, and spent much of December traveling to do interviews and meet my potential future employers. Here are my reflections from "Match Day":

This internship matching process is strange to say the least. The night before it happened, I thought to myself, "I think that it will be hard to find out where I am going—wherever that might be, because it means that I am not going to the other places that I really liked." To receive an email that says, "You have been matched to…"—an email that quite literally can change the course of your life. That one email, two sentences in length, tells you where you will be living for the next year.

It is difficult to describe my emotions upon getting that email. New Mexico was one of my top choices. In fact, it was my top choice in terms of the type of environment where I thought I would like to live. I had received a match at one of my top sites, so I should have been happy, right?! And yet…

I had ranked Children's Hospital of Philadelphia my #1. I knew all along that there was a chance I could be matched anywhere, and I knew that this was a competitive site, etc. But in my mind, somehow, I had envisioned myself there. They have a deaf program, and had seemed eager to have one of their interns participate in that. What I have come to realize over the last couple of days, was that what I truly had envisioned and a major aspect that I liked about that program was that its vicinity to D.C.

As I mourn the loss of the experiences I thought I might have there, I am realizing that most of it had to do with the friends that I would no longer live near. The idea of hoping on a train, or even just driving the 2 hours to see friends; to

stay for a weekend on "the island;" to collaborate with my advisor at Gallaudet—with whom I really enjoy meeting for coffee (or breakfast) and talking and
working and thinking and planning; to maybe fit in a game of racquetball at the
GWU gym on a Sunday; to visit my old home and favorite roommate in Takoma
Park; and to continue attending the monthly Eat the Planet gatherings with my
female friends—who are so refreshing and encouraging and wonderful. I liked
the idea of all of that, and I am continuing to mourn the loss of those opportunities. I know there are other ways—visits, phone calls, emails—which are great,
but not the same. Know that I will miss you.

When I think back to the time when I was applying for internships, I was
eager to go anywhere. I applied to sites in New Mexico, Minnesota, North Caro-
lina, even Canada. At that time, I was open-minded to going where the universe
might take me. I did not even apply to internship sites at all in D.C., so why do I
have the right to be disappointed that I don't get to live there? Part of the plan
was to go elsewhere, to see a different place, to spread my wings a little more. I
can't explain my emotions, only to try to describe them and work through them,
I guess.

It has now been a couple of days, and I have had time to think things over. I
am now excited about this next phase of my life. I was given the gift of perspective, "In a few months, after you have worked there, you will look back and know
that you could never have gone anywhere else and have the experiences that you
will be having because you went there. It will be just right for you. It will lead to
you to meet the people and make the connections you will need for the next
phase of your life and your career." I believe that this is true.

It took going back and re-reading the journal entry that I made immediately
after my trip to Albuquerque to remind myself of how much I liked it there, how
comfortable I felt in that space. Here are some of the things that I wrote:

The night before the interview: I had dinner in "old town." I met four people
tonight, all of whom were friendly and talked to me as if I were going to be their
close friend; only I didn't know it yet. The amazing thing was that each of these
people previously lived in D.C. All of them. They each told me of how they had
come to New Mexico, loved it, and decided not to leave. They described how the
"spirit of the place gets into your blood" and the beauty of the place "makes you
wonder how you ever lived any where else." I wondered on my way back to the
hotel, "Humm—I met four people tonight, all of them from D.C., all of them
eager to tell me why this was such a wonderful place to live. Is this a sign?"

On the plane, after the interview: I really like Albuquerque. The gorgeousness
of the blue sky, contrasted with the white of the adobe buildings make the land-

scape "stand out." You can see mountains all around, very near to town on the one side, and a bit farther in the distance on the other side—snow covered. The hiking trail is eight miles from the medical school campus. I feel good here. The guy who would be my advisor was great—very laid-back style, but clearly very intelligent and committed to working with adolescents. So many of the other internships advertise that they require 60 hours a week. The advisors here, and the intern that I had lunch with, said this is truly a 40-50 hour per week job. I am not afraid of working hard, but I really liked the relaxed atmosphere here. The people that interviewed me were great. I can imagine myself working with them. The training seems good, too. The population is a mixture of Hispanic, Native American and Anglo. The entire mix and feel of this place is different. The Medical School in Albuquerque serves the whole state and they are committed to providing culturally sensitive services for everyone, regardless of their ability to pay. I have to admit that I was impressed that the psychology department has a plane, to take psychologists and interns to other parts of the state to provide services. It seems fun and a bit exotic.

I checked out the "scene" a bit after the interview, and found an independent bookstore, an organic food co-op, and a store that was a combination stationary store/soda fountain/hairdresser. These were all very cool. I asked about the local live music scene and was told they have great music here, with lots of folk performers and blues musicians. Perfect! Just before I caught the bus to head to the airport, I saw a roadrunner—a real one. I could live here, I think, and be very happy.

So—I will head off to Albuquerque from Rome (a study in contrasts, you think?) and start my internship July 1st. It hit me yesterday that this is it—the last of the steps, hurdles, and milestones on my way to finishing what has felt at times, like the "all illusive Ph.D." in Clinical Psychology. I have one year left of internship and that is all. I thought about it when I defended my dissertation, but there was still having to apply to internships, interview, get placed somewhere…Now it feels different. My dissertation, my coursework, comprehensive exams, passing the sign language exam, all those tests, term papers, and reports—done. I start my internship in July in Albuquerque, New Mexico. One year later I will finally be Dr. Amy Szarkowski.

My sense of place

The feeling of being in Italy is changing. I am moving away from the excitement of turning the corner and finding something new each day. That excitement is being replaced by an equally delightful feeling of my sense of place. I no longer worry about getting lost. I have not seen every nook and cranny of the city, and there are many places that I have glanced over, or run by, and have not taken the time to really see them or know what they are about. I am still exploring. The difference is that now I know where I am. I have seen much of it before. I enjoying seeing the same places repeatedly and yet noticing new aspects of them each time. It is not all new, but it is becoming more comfortable. I will continue to explore and find new parts of the city, and new areas that I have missed. I will also continue to walk on the same streets on my way to and from work, getting to know the vendors at the fruit stands, and recognizing the newspaper guy on the corner of each intersection.

In the last week, I have been asked directions by 3 different people, and I could tell them how to get where they wanted to go. I didn't have to look at the map they were holding, and I didn't have to say, "No lo so" (I don't know). I would say, "Go straight for two blocks, then right, and take that past Piazza Barbarini and keep going straight for about 6 more blocks, and that puts you at Piazza Venezia. You will see the "wedding cake" statue. The road to the left of that is the Foro Imperial. Follow it and it runs right into the Coliseum." After they thanked me for my help, I responded, "Sure, no problem, happy to help."

Formal/Informal & Anna

I have trouble with this formal/informal part of the Italian language. I am fine with showing respect to my elders, such as the Seniora. Using the formal form in addressing a person I have just met feels natural to me as well. It is nice to meet someone, address them formally, and then, at some point, both persons agree to use the informal tense—it is a marker of closeness of that relationship, at least a level of comfortability with that person.

I am a foreigner in this land, using a language that is not my own. I am trying to show respect and "do it right." I want to follow the appropriate social norms and traditions. Sometimes, though, it is hard.

Anna, the security guard who worked on my floor, is the reason for my angst and difficulties with this topic. She is friendly and kind, and was welcoming to me from the first day I arrived to begin work at the CNR. We joke, laugh, and greet each other every day. She knows the events that are happening in my life, and is always asking about them. She sends me kind e-cards telling me that she likes having me in the office, and she brings me desserts that she has made. I appreciate the smiles that she brings to a workplace that is sometimes quite busy and hurried. I can take my written work to Anna, who will correct the Italian for me, before I pass it on to my superior. I appreciate this assistance so much, as it allows my precious time with my supervisor to be spent on issues of substance, and not on my sketchy Italian writing skills. Anna is the first to arrive and the last to leave, each and every day. She is a valuable asset to the group, as a security guard who also signs and is able to communicate with the various deaf individuals that are always visiting our building and working on various projects.

Anna has worked for the CNR for 9 years. Yet, she must refer to everyone that works there as "dotteressa" or "dottore." They refer to her simply as "Anna." I told Anna during my first week that I prefer she refer to me as "Amy." I did not want to use the formal tense with this woman that I have come to know and appreciate. I really, truly like her. How could I ask her refer to me formally, when it is I that go to her asking for assistance?

Several weeks ago, it was suggested that I do not "need" to talk to Anna. Indirectly, it was said that spending time with Anna was not necessary, that she is simply the security guard, after all. The following day, as I entered the building at the same time as my co-workers, and I greeted the man at the front door with a friendly, "Buon giorno"—I was told that I do not "need" to speak to him either. He just works there. I was struck by this, saddened. Are these not people? Do they not deserve respect for just being human beings? They have never been anything but kind to me, and I would not dream of being anything but kind in return. How could my "status" as a researcher in this building make me any more important than the guy that lets me in the door? Without him there, I couldn't work.

This "show of respect," it seems to me, is not a show of respect at all, in many cases. It feels more like a way of differentiating class, education, and social status. It is distancing and unkind. I am an American; "breaking the rules," I have been told. I suppose that, had I been raised in this culture, it might feel more natural to me. I am not sure about that, though. It does not seem right. I will not change the way that I interact with Anna, or with the other "workers" in my building. Would not a true sign of respect mean treating people equally?

15

La Vacanza in Italia

I mentioned before that I am independent. And I said that this could be difficult when in a relationship with me. Joe, the person I had been dating for several years, was on the other end of that. Going to Italy meant leaving him in the U.S. I have to thank him, though, for his amazing support during that time. I will always and forever cherish those times I spent with him.

It was nice to travel in Italy, near the end of my tenure there, and to share that space that had become sacred to me with someone so special to me. It was wonderful to know the language at that point and be able to be the "tour guide" and to share some of the magic this place had for me with someone who knew me and understood me. We saw amazing things and had a great time.

The arrival of Joe

Joe was here to visit!! I had not seen him in three months, so it was a sweet reunion, with lots of hugs and squeezes at the airport—heck, those hugs and squeezes just continued for the rest of the week! It was great to see him. He was here for 10 days, and I took vacation while he was here. We traveled around Italy and had a great time. Below is a description:

Torino & the Park

We stopped in Torino on our way to the mountains to have lunch at a park along the river. We rented a two-person bicycle for a half an hour, and toured the remainder of the park. It was a beautiful day, a Sunday, and there were many people laying in the grass, enjoying the spring weather and the company of their loved ones. In Italy, they make out like crazy—doesn't seem to matter who is around or watching.

Torino will be the home of the 2004 Winter Games. I thought it was neat to see the town, so that later, when I watch the games on TV, I can say, "I was there!" The town is at the foothills of some major mountains. It seemed like a great place for the Olympics to me.

Aosta and the Dolomites

After our stopover in Torino, we headed to Aosta, actually to the Valle D'Aosta, in the further most area of Northwestern Italy. This town, for centuries, was part of France. It wasn't until about 140 years ago that the borders of Italy were established as we know them. The town is bilingual—with signs in both French and Italian, and with people speaking a little of this, a little of that. This added a certain element of foreignness for me, which I enjoyed. Although I was traveling in Italy, which is "home to me now," this felt like I was going to a foreign land.

We stayed at a charming place, whose owner lives in the house above the two rooms that she rents out for the night. Our room was situated aside a tiny courtyard, down an alley, off a little street. Charming. We were struck at how different this seemed, with its antiques laying about, compared to the feeling one gets at a Motel 6, where the TV remote is bolted to the nightstand. It was lovely, as was the owner, who gave us a $30 discount at the end of our stay because, as she said, "You are just so nice. I would like to do something nice for you."

The first night in this quaint place, we ate at a restaurant on the edge of town. Our waiter was an interesting older gentleman who took a great deal of pride in the food that was served. He encouraged us to try the local specialties, which we did (not knowing what we were ordering, and we got a plate of raw/cured meats—not the best thing for a used-to-be vegetarian, but...). After a lovely dinner, he treated us to an after dinner liquor. I was so pleased with the generosity and realness of the people that lived in this town.

Mt. Pila

On our first day trip, Joe and I rode a funivila (cable car) up to Mt. Pila. This granted us great views of the surrounding mountains as we rode up to the starting point of our hike. Mt. Pila is also a ski hill, and people were indeed skiing, though the snow was melting quickly and there were dry patches to be found under many of the trees. We had looked at a map and planned a route. The trail was difficult to find. When we found what we thought was the trail, it bisected a ski run, and was unsafe to follow. I had witnessed some of those skiers, especially the newbies, flapping and flailing their way down the hill. We decided to venture off and follow our instincts, which lead us to nice pastures and more incredible views. The spring flowers, many of which were purple, were sprouting through the light layer of snow, determined to reach the sunshine. We had packed a lunch, and shared it while lying on the grass and admiring the peaks. The air felt free, my lungs clean. This day was not what I might call "breath-taking," it was more like "breath-giving."

The mountains at sunrise

I awoke early and set out on my own to capture the sun and the beauty of my surroundings on film. It was dark when I set out—I watched the world change before my eyes, from a sleepy small town in a valley surrounded by dark mountains, to a sunny community situated in the valley, with mountains on three sides. There was not a single cloud in the sky. The rising sun reflected off of the pure white snow on the mountains, making the entire valley appear pink, then orange, followed by a yellow glow that remained until nearly mid-morning. It felt truly peaceful.

I walked the length and the width of this tiny town that morning, exploring and noting interesting places that I hoped to return to, after the rest of the world woke up and the shops were opened. The streets were narrow—the town was build long, long before the advent of the automobile. In fact, there are records of people living in the Valle d'Aosta for 7000 years. This area has been used as a passage between Italy, and the lands to the North for centuries, for millennia. The Roman empire used this passage to expand, and Napoleon used the same passage in pushing the Romans back. One of the passes is known as the Saint Bernard Pass—for the dog. Despite its beauty, natural habitat, and gorgeous landscapes, this area is the least populated in all of Italy. The main jobs involve agriculture, raising the cows that provide the milk and cream for the food of this region, as well as producing fontaine cheese—known throughout Italy and various other parts of the world.

Since the roads are so narrow, no cars are permitted in the center—allowing for a community feel that, in my opinion, is unbeatable. It is wonderful to walk, to stop when something catches your eye, to wonder and explore without waiting for the cars to pass. I witnessed the café owners arriving at their work, slowly opening the shutters, and saying, "Buona giornata" or "Bon Jour" to the members of their town.

No one was in a hurry, there was nothing that was so important that would prevent any of him or her from taking the time to speak to his or her neighbors. I watched an older couple interact with a younger man in his 40s, who was making them coffee. They hugged him and kissed him on either cheek, asking about his family and his home. He responded and then returned the questions in kind. Then, the older woman said, "Yesterday you told us...." I was struck by the fact that this couple had talked to this man the day before, and yet the very next day, they were happy to see him again.

I understand some of the drawbacks of a small town. I know that once a person has been "labeled" it is often difficult to change the perception of others. Some people feel trapped by their small surroundings. Small towns can be limiting in the sense that they tend to not expose young people to different ways of living. But...the town were I grew up was very small, yet at times I find that I truly miss that sense of community that does not seem possible in larger cities. There may not be "exciting" things happening in some of these sleepy small towns, but there are people who know you, care about you, and want to be connected to you. Community can be a very good thing.

So close to France and Switzerland....

Joe and I went to the end of the line on the train—just kilometers from France. We saw Monte Bianco, known to most of the world as Mont Blanc. This large mountain straddles the border of Italy and France—though in both language it is known as "White Mountain," always covered with snow, and standing above the other large peaks that make up the Alps. We could see the Matterhorn, the largest mountain in the Swiss Alps, which seemed close enough that you could just touch it. We saw a large spire that was so steep it seemed the snow was unable to cling to it, since it was the only bare peak in the chain. It was titled "Il Dente del Gigante"—the Tooth of the Giant. It was definitely Joe's favorite. Each time he took in the vista, he contemplated what it would be like to summit those peaks. Unfortunately for him, I am not an ice climber—so ice picking my way up to one of the tallest mountains in the earth while crossing a glacier of solid ice, in avalanche season, was out of the question. Rock climbing, hiking, trekking, camping, backpacking—yes! Ice climbing, placing an axe in water (albeit frozen) to hold my weight and prevent me from plummeting thousands of meters—nope.

We spent the day hiking in a canyon and then climbed a mountain. The canyon was narrow, with massive rocks and white water, which must have carved this space between the two mountains over the course of millions and millions of years. In addition to the snowmelt, this stream is comprised of water from warm springs, which for centuries were used for medicinal purposes. The trail along the river, while beautiful, was made up of many small, tumbling rocks. We went to see the river, and noticed this trail, though we did not know where it went, we were just exploring a bit. We hiked in a short way, enjoyed the view, and turned back, deciding, instead, to climb one of the mountains around us, in search of the best views of the Dolomites.

The trail we chose was nice, steep, and diverse. We hiked through several different types of ecological environments while we ascended, from dense brush to tall trees, from sandstone to volcanic rock. Joe, having just finished a course in ecology (in which he got an "A" and an "Excellent" on his final paper!) was having a good time teaching me things I didn't know about my natural surroundings. He was cute.

The peak was elusive to us. Rather than the trail going to the top of the mountain we were on, it circled around the side. We continued on a trail for several hours, enjoying the panorama and sharing our love of the outdoors. When we reached an old, abandoned sheepherder's cottage, we stopped for our lunch of bread and fontaine cheese, made right there in that valley. We headed back on the same trail, stopped in town for some liquids—an entire liter of water between the two of us, in addition to the fruit juice we had just drank. We caught our train back to Aosta for another evening "on the town" before saying good-bye to the Italian Alps.

Cinque Terre—beautiful cliffs, wonderful seafood, brilliant lemons, and a nice hike

Cinque Terre is a place, actually five towns, on the Liguarian Sea on the Western coast of Italy. I have been hearing about this place since I arrived, people asking, "When are you going to Cinque Terre? You have to go there before you leave." Although I knew it might be a bit crowded this time of year, especially with the Italian tradition of taking a week (or two) of vacation around the Easter holiday. That was my chance, though, and it sounded like a nice place to take a visitor. We arrived in the evening, after a full day of traveling on trains. It was nice to stretch our legs and walk around a bit. We stayed in the town of Montarosso, the northern most of the 5 towns that span a short distance along the coast. Until about 50 years ago, these towns were only accessible by foot and by the sea. Today, there are still no roads for cars between the cities, though the rail line is available to carry the tourists into and out of the area.

We set out that evening to go for a jog together, though the trail was steep, with lots of stairs, which lead to more of a fast walk up the hill than a run. Still, it was beautiful. We watched the sunset from above, onto the small town we would be staying in that evening. The town was painted in bright, coral-type colors, the kind that attract the sun and seems to set off the beauty of the land around it. It was so wonderful to hug this person that I love, doing one of the things that I most love to do—watching the sunset. It felt magical to me.

We decided to set out early the next morning to begin our hike. We had read that it takes about 5 hours to walk between the towns, on the trails that pass through olive groves, and lemon and fig trees. The lemons were a brilliant yellow, sharing their fragrance with us as we passed. I loved the contrast of the bright yellow against the deep green of the leaves, offset by the sea blue of the water and the slate gray of the rocky cliffs. Photos cannot to justice to the feelings created in the presence of that kind of beauty. The area between the northern-most towns, where we were, was the most beautiful. During this part of our hike, we were alone, to enjoy the world as she woke up, opened her eyes, and smiled on us. The weather was cool in the morning, perfect for hiking up steep terrain, yet sunny and beautiful, beckoning us to be outside, drinking in the rays of sunshine.

Other people were hitting the trails in the late morning, and we ran into them toward the end of our hike. The views were still nice, and the last two towns were nice, though the latter portion was not as challenging and close to nature as it had been in the beginning of our jaunt. The trail was busy, with people frequently passing each other. We took the train back to Monterosso, and decided to go for a walk on the beach.

The beaches in Cinque Terre were made up of pebbles, not sand. My wimpy feet had difficulty traversing the beach from the blanket to the water. We brought our books, drawing pads, writing paper, and cameras, and spent time on the beach enjoying the sights and our experience of being there. We each went our own way for a while, thinking our own thoughts. We came back together again for dinner.

I know I talk about food a lot, but this is Italy, and it is important. In order to relay my experiences, I have to mention the food. Joe ordered an appetizer of mussels. When it arrived, it was as large as a soup pot, filled with mussels. We both thought it was an error, telling the waiter that he had ordered that for an appetizer, not his main meal. We were slightly embarrassed when he showed us the menu—those muscles, indeed, were the appetizer. During our time in Cinque Terre, we ate seafood every chance we had. The next evening, we shared a seafood pasta dinner, which was filled with seafood, in every bite. There were whole prawns, with the heads on, and shellfish that I did not even recognize. Calamari, fresh, could be found in the pasta as well. It was truly delicious.

Touring Rome on Easter weekend

Joe and I got back to Rome on Good Friday in the late evening. We cooked at home (we needed to after all those seafood dinners) and relaxed after being gone for the week. We set out on Saturday to do some exploring of Rome. Joe had not been here before. The first day he was in town, we walked around near the coliseum, but other than that he had not seen any of the city. We wandered around the Foro Imperiali, Piazza Venezia, Capitoline Hill, and the Isola Tibertina. We wandered into Trastevere, where we had lunch outside before walking north to the Vatican.

St. Peter's is amazing. Each time that I see it, I am struck by how grand it is, by the fact that so many people make a pilgrimage to this sight each year, and by the fact the there are so many works of art in this one place. We witnessed the decorating for the next day, Easter, and the preparations of the festivities that would follow.

We walked to the Castle St. Angel, bought some ice cream, and lay in the grass in the park surrounding the castle. It was a nice way to pass the afternoon, laying in each other's arms and sharing out thoughts in the sunshine. On the walk home, we stopped by Piazza Navona and the Pantheon. All in all, it was a great day.

Sunday, Joe and I went for a long run, seeing more of the city, the various fountains, and running through the Villa Borghese. The day seemed to pass much too quickly, as we both knew he would be leaving the next morning. We slept in, went for a walk around the neighborhood, and hugged a lot.

16

On Leaving

On leaving

It is happening again. Maybe you know this feeling I am taking about—the feeling of leaving a place that you have, in whatever way, claimed as your own. The feeling of "ahhhh..." when looking back on the time you spent in a place. It is the desire to secure every part of it in your memory, so that you never lose what it is that you gained while you were there. I know that Italy will remain with me, in my thoughts and in the way it has changed the way that I think, also in my heart and in the way that my heart has been touched by the lives of the people who have shared this experience with me. The language, or rather the knowledge that I have the ability to learn a new language—has opened new doors to the way that I view myself. This place has given me confidence in handling difficult situations and taught me to appreciate the beauty in my surroundings. I am leaving Rome, but taking so much of it along with me. I am changed because I have been here. Now I have to say farewell....

This feeling is also the desire to drink it all in, to live more fully in those last moments, to cherish it, to savor it, with the knowledge that it is coming to an end. When you are getting ready to leave a place, you think about the things you have done, and you make a mental list of the things you still must accomplish before you leave. "What is it that I want to be sure to do?" you might ask yourself. I don't believe in regrets, I don't want to look back on my time and think, "I should have done...." There is a sense of urgency—what have I not done that I want to do while I still can? There is conflict though, for along with this urgency is the feeling of wanting to "just be." I have seen many ruins; will I even remember if I see one more? There is the desire to people-watch, to be a part of the crowd, to sit in a café and ponder what it has been like to live in Italy, to not do anything other than my normal routine out of a desire to keep it just as it is for as long as I can.

This feeling—the need for closure—involves not only saying good-bye to those you have met, as if you were going away on a vacation, but to say good-bye with the knowledge that it will never again be the same. You may visit, or they may visit you, and you can continue to grow in your friendship in a myriad of ways, but it will never again be the same. You know this deep inside, as you say your good-byes. You are positive that there are some who will stay in your life, just as surely as there are those who will serve only as part of your memories of this place. You can cherish them as well, for without them this time would not have been the same, though you know that in saying good-bye, it means the end.

The end of a chapter means the beginning of another. It is with reflection on what has just happened, savoring those last words and pictures, that I slowly, slowly turn the page and look forward to the next adventure...

17

Lessons Learned

Some thoughts, reflections, and observations from Italy:

- People from other countries think that Americans have a "thing" about cleanliness, specifically regarding showering and body odors. Italians perceive body odor as natural. I will give them that to some extent…but I have to say that I think dandruff is yucky. It might be a cultural thing, and I am admitting my biases here, but if you have huge white flakes all over your clothes, my tendency is to think you should wash them off!

- We Americans tend to think of our country's history as being within the last 300 years. The Romans know what happened on this very land 2300 years ago. I wonder what if might have been like had "we" not eradicated the people who lived in the present day USA, and included their history in the making of our own. What a rich history that might have been…

- The Sunday afternoon "passagiata" is a good thing. If we all took one day a week to truly rest, to go out and be in the community, and to go for long walks and chat with friends and loved ones, I think we would all be happier.

- Tiramisu—you know, the dessert—well, here is an interesting bit for you: It means "to raise you up"—1. literally, like to give you a lift, or to pick you up 2.in the desert sense, as in it has a lot of caffeine and can "get you going," and 3.in the erotic sense—it also means "to get you aroused" or "to have a stiff penis." Think of that the next time you eat in an Italian restaurant!

- Piazzas are great—general, open spaces for people to gather to share the day. Locals and tourists alike congregate to see how "the Italians" live. Why do so many places in the U.S. not plan a place for people to congregate? Why do the high school kids have to hang out at the 7-11 parking lot these days?

- Studying something makes you realize how much you don't know. I am working on Italian now, and that makes me more aware not only of what I don't know in terms of Italian verb conjugations and the like, but about how many languages there are—how many people think and talk and work differently than I. It makes me feel small, and gives me good perspective. Yet, it has opened up a whole new world for me—which makes me feel bigger than life. Next might be Spanish, then maybe French, or am I brave enough to try Chinese?? Well...

- Poop laws are good things. If your dog poops, you should have to clean it up. In a city with lots of dogs and no laws, poop abounds.

- Some thoughts on oil.

If Americans paid the true price of oil, the entire U.S. relationship with the Middle East would change. I believe it would help to resolve many of the issues of we currently face there.

In a place where the people have pay the REAL price of gas, people are more conscious of their choices—whether to drive or take public transportation. I was in a tiny car with someone recently—the car averages 70 miles to the gallon. It cost 55 Euro to fill it up. She is a well-to-do woman, yet only drives when necessary because of the cost of gas. In Rome, it costs $25 for a transportation pass that will allow you to use the metro, the buses, and the tram—any kind of public transportation—for a month.

SMART cars first appeared when I was in Italy 3 yrs ago, now they are everywhere. The 110+ miles to the gallon that they get puts my Echo to shame.

- If the USA constantly tears things down to build new ones, we will never have a rich archeological history. Rather than see old buildings as "old" I think it would be nice to build them sturdier and maintain them. Just as with people, older doesn't mean worse—it just might mean wiser.

- It is nice to not have to pay to sit down in a restaurant. In Italy, the price for a standing lunch is half the price of the sitting lunch. There is something to be said for the US notion of sitting down to eat (even if we don't take advantage of this and often "sit down" to eat in our cars).

- Italian men treat their mothers with a great deal of respect and adoration. They are known for their close relationships with their moms, and typically continue to live with their mothers until they are married, and sometimes even after. Had Catholicism not been rooted in Rome (speaking loosely here of course)—how might the story of Mary and Joseph been different? Mary sure gets a lot of credit. How about a guy who willingly took in a wife that was pregnant and raised a child that was reportedly not his? Just a thought....

- Make-up and fancy hair might help to make a woman look younger, but it doesn't cover up the effects of long-term smoking on the face. I promise.

- In the last week I have received the same advice for 3 Italians, "Make sure you eat a lot of vegetables. Pizza tends to plug you up." In each case, this was unsolicited information.

- Who says you have to pay a lot for good wine? The corner market sells Moltipulciano red wine for $1.56 (that is actually euro, not dollar, but I don't know how to make that sign). Either way—it is just slightly more expensive than buying water, and it is GOOD.

- At my new "casa" there was a huge, old TV that didn't work well. The first day, my roommate and I decided that we didn't want the TV out, so we put it in storage. It is *amazing* to me how much time I have to do other things, when I would have normally been watching TV—and I was not one to watch a lot of TV in the first place. I have to say, it is very nice. To those who say they never have enough time, or that it is difficult to get things done, I suggest not turning on your TV. Try it for a week. I have read more books and done more exploring, and *chosen* how to spend my time, rather than letting the TV dictate what I do. It feels freeing.

- Admittedly, the TV-free thing is easier since the Italian programming sucks. The near-naked ladies dancing in every single show didn't do that much for me. But for some of you, I know that not understanding what they are saying may not be enough of a deterrent.

- Did you know that Italians have good chocolate? Yep—Perugina, a chocolate manufacturer, is located in the next region over from Lazio, where I live. They make Baci (kisses)—with chocolate and hazelnuts. Hershey's stole the idea from them, I think, because these kisses have been around for a long time. Part of me wishes I didn't like their chocolate so much, but part the other part of me...well, I really like the stuff!

- Running is my rebellion. You know the saying, "When in Rome, do as the Romans do." I am trying to adapt to the culture here and to not stand out as a tourist or foreigner—at least not all the time. But running is my refuge. The fact that no one does it here won't make me stop. I get stared at frequently. I receive glances that seem to say, "You are a crazy American." I feel better when I run. Besides, I think the real reason that Italian woman don't run is because running shoes don't have high enough heels.

- I want to clarify something. In my last letter I mentioned that I don't know anyone *like* President Bush. I was not trying to indicate that I didn't know *anyone who likes* him; obviously people do and have supported him. I meant that I don't personally know any people that are like him, referring more to the money and power that he wields—his world and mine are quite different. I know that opinions vary, and I respect that your opinions about some of the things that I wrote about might be different, even the opposite of mine. That is fine, and I would encourage dialogue about that. In no way am I attempting to state that my views are the right ones or the only ones out there. Heck, my views have changed drastically in the 6 months that I have been here, and I reserve the right for them to change again, many times over, as I grow and change and learn more. Please accept my thoughts for what they are—my thoughts and ponderings now, in this space where I am.

- I missed French toast. Sure, they have eggs and bread here, but the bread has lots of holes and isn't right for French toast. And what is French Toast without maple syrup?

- St. Valentine's Day is certainly celebrated in Italy—but I didn't find a single card, or a box of candy. I was looking, too. I thought I might send out cards to love ones, and I thought I might buy myself a box of candy at 50% off on the "day after"—but it wasn't possible. Hum—seems it is just about telling people that you care about them, and not what you should buy them that matters here. Novel idea, huh?

- I enjoyed hearing some of the reactions to my last "edition." I learned that one person used to work with Michael Moore in Flint, Michigan, that another had his own "umbrella story" and more than one of you knew exactly what I was talking about with the colonoscopy experience. I like that.

- Towels take a long time to dry if you don't have a clothes dryer.

- We shouldn't discourage art. In the U.S., generally, I think we do. "Artists are poor." We don't view being an artist as a good way to make a living, and we tend to think that artists are lazy and don't want "real jobs." Maybe we should all pick up some crayons, or some play-doh and remember that art used to be fun. I am *not* one to preach on this topic at all. I didn't take art classes; instead I took the academic route. It got me where I am today, and I am not complaining. I just think that I, we, need more balance. Being in Italy reminds me frequently that art, creation, and expression are good things. I may not be another Michelangelo, or Leonardo da Vinci, but I bet I can sculpt a play-doh dinosaur. Even if you can't tell what it is, I will know, and I will have created it. By the way, did you know that "da Vinci" was not Leonardo's last name? It means "from Vinci"—the town he lived in.

- What is it about pinching my cheeks? I didn't like it as a kid, and especially don't like it now. I am 29 years old. I get my cheeks pinched here at least 3 times a week. The Italians don't hold back when describing physical features. For example, they have no qualms about telling people that they have a big nose, or that they are gaining weight. They also have no problem at all telling me that I have big cheeks, and then they squeeze them. Hard. And they don't let go for a long time. I showed a co-worker a picture of my family, and she commented that we all have those cheeks—and then she pinched mine extra times, to make up for those she doesn't get to pinch for my sister or brothers.

- Italian Chinese food and American Chinese food are NOT the same. I have just learned that Indian food in Italy is not the same as Indian food in America either. Just curious—what does Chinese food taste like in China? What about Indian food in India? Thai food is my favorite, but I haven't been to Thailand—would it be at all the same there? Would it still be my favorite??

- I went to an art opening at a gallery with another Fulbright student, herself an artist. I met some great people there, all of them artists as well. They were fun, we chatted, laughed, and went out for wine afterward. None of them had enough money to buy any art from the other artists. If the only people that generally go to gallery openings, how do artists make any money?

- I was in a movie. Yep, just today, I was filmed for a movie. Whether or not I will make the finished cut, I don't know. This happened once before, when I first arrived, and I accidentally walked through the set, not knowing it was being filmed (the "set" was my street). Today was funny, though. The director said, "You American, yes? Yes, of course, because you running. Can you running here un ultra volta (another time)?" I pointed to the street I had just been on, and he nodded an enthusiastic "Yes!" Sure, no problem. After running on the same street three times, he told me that he was finished with me. He said, "We not know where to find a person running. That person needs to look like American runner, and we not know. Then here you are, running!" He beamed. It won't make me a movie star—but it seemed to make his day, which was good enough for me. But I do wish I had gotten the name of the film, darn…

- For the record, Italian food is not only pasta, cheese, wine, and olive oil. There are also several other items that I had not previously associated with Italy, but I see them here all the time: 1) Eggplant—you find it everywhere, 2) Artichoke—available on pizza at every pizzeria, 3) Hazelnuts—especially in Baci (chocolates) and gelato, 4) Fungi porcini—mushrooms. All over the place.

- If pasta is starchy and causes you to gain weight, why are all these Italian women so skinny? I don't buy it. Bring on the penne!

- Italian bills come every 2-3 months or so. Things like the electric and gas bills—they come sometimes and not others. You pay them when you get them. No comment really—just something I find amazing.

- All of the bakeries make a special dessert for the Feast of St. Joseph. It is a pastry puff filled with cream and it is delicious. These are made only on this day, I am told. Makes me think I should learn all the saint day and know when to hit the bakeries...

- Running is my rebellion. You know the saying, "When in Rome, do as the Romans do." I am trying to adapt to the culture here and to not stand out as a tourist or foreigner—at least not all the time. But running is my refuge. The fact that no one does it here won't make me stop. I get stared at frequently. I receive glances that seem to say, "You are a crazy American." I feel better when I run. Besides, I think the real reason that Italian woman don't run is because running shoes don't have high enough heels.

- Milan in particular, and Italy in general, are known for being trendsetters in fashion. They "new looks" are chosen over a year in advance. One problem here is that clothes are not selling this spring. It is creating a "crisis" in the economy. Why? The fashion for this spring are camouflage—it is all over, in ever store, and no one is buying it. Interesting.

- The term "grande culo" in Italian means "good fortune." Literally, it means, "big butt." Somehow, I don't think this would fly in the U.S. Having my share of "curves"—a.k.a. a round butt that sticks out a lot (in fact, I was once told by an African-American co-worker that, if I were Black, I would be "hot" but since I was White, I would be considered "plump." Nice.) Anyway, I find it hard to believe that this term means good fortune. If that is what the Italians think—I am OK with that!

- You should never assume that, just because you got a hotel room and did not stay in a hostel, that your room actually has a shower or a toilet. That would be an error on your part.

- In the US, when a good-looking, well-dressed man passes, women often wonder if he is gay. I know this is stereotyping and way over-generalizing, but there seems to be some truth there. Here in Italy, they wonder if he is a priest. I was on the bus the other, an attractive man walked by, and the three woman behind me began discussing his appearance, and then one said, "You know, all the good-looking ones are priests."

- I miss coffee shops. Don't get me wrong, there are at least 2 million bars in Rome (I am estimating, but I am sure that is pretty close) in which you can get coffee, but they are the "stand at the bar, gulp it down, and leave" kind of places. I am looking for a place to go when I want to write—when I don't want to be at home (or when being home just isn't that productive—there are dishes to do, laundry to hang, toilets to clean—ok, I am teasing about the last one, the toilets never stopped me from doing anything, but you get the idea). What I am doing is not really "work" to be done at my office. I haven't found a place like that. It makes me appreciate my old hang out for that kind of work, Savory's, even more.

- I am not a huge fan of dogs. If you have been around them and me at the same time, you already know this. I tell myself, "Don't be afraid, they can smell fear." I repeat in my head, "The owners love the dog, they must be OK." Why is it that all dog owners say, "My dog never bites." Well, some do—I have been bitten more than a few times. The most recent event happened two days ago—yet another dog bite! This one didn't break the skin—not where the dog bit me anyway. The other side of my body, where I crashed into a motorino trying to escape the jaws of the ferocious animal—that is another story. It did break the skin, and gave me quite a bruise. I had been out on a run, and had to walk the rest of the way home because my leg hurt so badly. The owner of that dog, too, said, "My dog doesn't usually bite." Thanks, Dude, but "doesn't usually" isn't good enough for me. Tell it to someone who will believe you....

- Just imagine my fear when I learned that Pescara was having the annual Carabinieri convention while I was there. Yikes!

- I am struck by the fact that most Italians that I meet are content. It is pleasant to be around people who are happy with what they have, and who want to enjoy life. Although of course there are exceptions, so many of the Italians that I know are not striving to achieve some great thing, they want to have the time to enjoy their families, their food, their homes and the beauty around them. There is something very nice about that simplicity of purpose.

- Let's see—Holy Thursday, Good Friday, and Easter Monday are holidays. April 25th is a Liberation Day—a holiday, as is May 1st, which falls on a Thursday, so we might as well take Friday the 2nd off as well. When should we go back to work?

- Diet plans always tell you to substitute fruit for sweets. Right, like you will chose that apple over the apple pie, right? But in Italy, fruit is served last and is viewed as dessert. I am starting to think that fruit can serve as that after-dinner sweet I need. Of course, if faced with the option of Better-than-sex-chocolate-cake, or an orange, well…but If I am not given the choice, fruit does seem to work as a filler-upper after the meal. Not that one needs to fill up after an Italian meal, but just in case….

- They are working on the street in front of my house. By hand, they pull out the cobblestones and work on the pipe under the road and then replace the stones, again doing this by hand. I was told by one of the workers that the spaces between the rocks allow for the absorption of water, reducing problems with run-off and allowing the water to be put back into the water table. Doing it by hand isn't "backward" after all. This same guy took a nap in his wheelbarrow for about 30 minutes that afternoon. I liked him very much.

0-595-29665-3